HOUSE OF CESSNA BOOK II

With Commentaries

By

C W Cissna

A Reprisal of the work done by Howard Cessna and published in 1935, with additions of newly discovered information.

Privately Published
Albuquerque, NM
September 2011

Do You Have These Books in Your Family History Library?

$8.00 each

Our Fifteen Minutes   *2012*

A collection of humorous, sad and inspiring newspaper articles spot lighting Cessna/Cissna/Cisney family members in moments of fame and infamy, over a 200 year period.

www.createspace.com/3791886

Bury My Children in A Strange Land   *2011*

A dramatized history of John and Stephen Cessna who follow their father (Jean du Cesne) from Ireland to a new land, this is the story of how our family came to this country.   **www.createspace.com/3772272**

Forgotten Courage   *2011*

Thrilling scenes of the American Revolution are portrayed in the story of how Stephen Cessna/Cissna struggled to be a Patriot in every part of his life. A heroic common man tossed in the storm of national politics, he was among the first Americans to suffer PTSD or "Battle Fatigue".

www.createspace.com/3663152

The Reluctant American   *2010*

Captured and adopted by the Pottawatomie Indians, Captain Joseph Cessna/Cissna protected his family and neighbors in the bloodiest part of the Revolution. He knew Chief Pontiac, Tecumseh and other great warriors.

www.createspace.com/3644874

Let Me Live in Peace   *2012*

The life of Col. Charles Cessna, a Patriot caught in bitter politics after the Revolution. His determination and courage helped to open frontier settlements in Pennsylvania, Georgia, Kentucky and Mississippi.

www.createspace.com/3896573

COMMENTARY:

This volume is a digital scan; of a 30 year old photo copy; of a 50 year old micro film; of a 20 year old copy of Howard Cessna's book published in 1935. It had a very limited printing and it has been difficult for most people to get a copy. In the text, he states that it is his wish for future generations to use this material to continue their historical search. Every member of this great family owes an enormous debt of gratitude for his work and sacrifice. He was the first of our family's historians.

That being said, there are qualifications to be made to his work. Hence comes the writing of the commentary version. Travel and research were very difficult in the late 1800's. Our century has afforded many more opportunities for uncover facts. Local Historical Societies have produced indexes of land, court, marriage, death, cemetery and other records. Many long lost books have been digitized by Google and it is possible to look in places that Howard Cessna did not have access to.

Commentary pages have been inserted along with his original work to point researchers in a clearer direction. No criticism is intended of our benefactor, Howard Cessna. We all start with his work, and pursue a clearer understanding of history.

CONTENTS

I. ALL CESSNAS ARE INDEBTED TO MRS. VAN EVERA ... 9

II. THE FAMILY COAT OF ARMS—DECESSNA ... 11

III. TABLET TO REVOLUTIONARY HERO ... 17

IV. TWO PUPS ... 29

V. ARCHIVES AND OTHER RECORDS ... 32

VI. CAN YOU EXPLAIN THE FOLLOWING? ... 37

VII. JOHN CESSNA II FARM ... 40

VIII. CESSNAS OF YAZOO CITY, MISS. ... 42

IX. EARLY COURT RECORD AND ROBERT CESSNAS DESCENDANTS ... 43

X. JAMES CESSNA, BROTHER OF MAJ. JOHN CESSNA; HIS WILL, HIS FATHER'S WILL AND NAMES OF DESCENDANTS ... 64

XI. STEPHEN CESSNA, BROTHER OF MAJ. JOHN CESSNA—HIS DESCENDANTS ... 81

XII. CAPTAIN SAMUEL T. WILLIAMS, A DESCENDANT OF SQUIRE JAMES CESSNA IV ... 101

XIII. DESCENDANTS OF SEVERAL BRANCHES OF THE CESSNA FAMILY ... 105

XIV. HISTORY ... 127

XV. AUTOBIOGRAPHY OF HOWARD CESSNA ... 136

XVI. LETTERS FROM MRS. BECK, MT. PLEASANT, MICH. AND MRS. MORGAN, AMES, IOWA ... 176

XVII. OBITUARIES ... 178

XVIII. FRENCH HISTORY OF CESSNA'S ... 189

XIX. PRESENT ADDRESS (1935) OF CESSNAS ... 196

ILLUSTRATIONS

Page

MR. HOWARD CESSNA..Frontispiece

THE FAMILY COAT OF ARMS.. 10

MAJOR JOHN CESSNA TABLET, CUMBERLAND ROAD........... 16

DEDICATION OF TABLET TO REVOLUTIONARY HERO........... 19

THE HONORABLE JOHN CESSNA.................................. 23

THE CESSNA HOMESTEAD NEAR RAINSBURG, PA................ 28

DR. ORANGE HOWARD CESSNA....................................179

PREFACE

In 1903 I had printed "The House of Cessna" after some ten years of research work which included names, &c., of the Cessnas of whom I had any record.

In that book I stated that it was my intention to later in life revise my work and include therein the History of the Cessnas in France. Being disappointed in not going to Europe in the past thirty years is largely the cause of writing this book which, in short, means—Cessna Genealogical Data obtained since writing The House of Cessna.

I feel it would be a great injustice to not only the present, but oncoming generations of the Cessnas to allow the information which has come to me in the past thirty years to be destroyed by fire or otherwise not made available.

The Institute of American Genealogy, Dearborn Street, Chicago, Ill., appointed me as their Bedford County Co-representative and the letters received from people all over the country interested in their ancestors causes me to feel assured that Cessnas will be indebted to any one giving them information.

Thousands of individuals are devoting their entire time in this country looking up ancestoral records; scores of Cessnas have joined the Sons and Daughters of American Revolution. The reader of these lines may not be interested, but on a guess, if a parent, the next generation and the one following will.

There are but six methods of tracing ones line of descent, viz.: Court Records, Bible Records, Tombstone, Church Records, by Parents Recollection and Archives or History.

Someone has said that in the death of any old citizen in any community, a portion of the local history has been lost.

Our early ancestors did not deem it necessary to keep a Diary, hence much that would now be appreciated is lost forever.

If my data as herein contained proves of assistance to any Cessna descendant in tracing their line of descent, I shall be repaid and it's that thought that prompts me to publish this Book.

I have added some reminiscences which are similar to an autobiography through a desire that the reader may know better the author.

Briefly, when you consider there were some eight or ten Cessnas connected with the frontier warfare and the Revolutionary War, and all descendants anxious to identify their relationship to one or the other and all writing me for information, you will see I unintentionally became sort of a clearing house for information. Hence I take this means to acquaint one and all of facts received.

Delay in publishing this book has been due largely to waiting for a reply from Europe concerning Cessnas there and to cost or price asked by publishers for printing this Book.

CHAPTER I

All Cessnas Are Indebted to Mrs. Van Evera

Every Cessna is deeply indebted to my much esteemed cousin —Mrs. Eleanor Cessna Van Evera for procuring our Coat of Arms which was secured after years of search and at a cost of several hundred dollars.

From this description any descendant will be able to have a painting such as Mrs. Van Evera presented to me which is framed and hangs on the wall just above the sword Major John Cessna used in the Revolutionary War.

The sword was obtained last year from Mr. Nave of Cumberland Valley. Mrs. Nave was an adopted daughter of Samuel Cessna, a grandson of Major John Cessna.

John De Cessna of Newark, Ohio, in company with his father, brought to my home couple years past, the most attractive horn I ever saw. Mr. Cessna, Sr., said he had ridden in his younger days fifty miles to obtain it from a Cessna, claiming it was used by Major John Cessna. It was around sixteen inches long, large, glossy and contained carvings picturing Forts and Stockades, Soldiers, etc.

Mr. Cessna was of that type we all like—quick to see a joke —and having discovered my interest in the horn, pretended to his son before leaving that he should examine the satchel for the powder horn. I don't recall ever having swiped anything, but had that horn been in the keeping of some other than a Cessna, I might have been tempted.

CHAPTER II

The Family Coat of Arms—De Cessna

FOREWORD

Heraldry is inspirational in its teaching and its symbolism is compelling, wherein lies its chief value. To bear coat-armour worthily involves obligations which cannot be avoided in honour.

A shield of Arms is an hereditary possession. It can be neither bought nor sold, but descends from father to son in every generation. It proclaims the gentleman and the lady in the true and exact definition of those terms (see Blackstone's "Commentaries," I, 406). Emblazoned upon it are the marks of recognition of valour, fortitude and merit won by those of our blood who have gone before, and to whom, under God, we owe our very existence. They treasured this shield, with its appropriate devices, beyond all other earthly possessions and were ever careful to observe the most honorable conduct, to friend and foe alike, so as to cast no blot or stain upon the escutcheon of which they were so justly proud.

This same shield of Arms, borne by the Esquire of the twentieth century and by his family, should be equally esteemed and cherished. To be true to the teachings of its symbolic figures, and to safeguard fully its honour and dignity, it is necessary that its bearer cultivate and practice the cardinal Christian virtues as a true Chevalier; that he have faith, reverence and courage; that he is entirely loyal to country, family and friends; that he be industrious; generous as his means permit; and patient under such trials and tribulations as will inevitably come to him. For a gentleman of coat-armour to disregard such principles of conduct, or to take improper advantage of another in professional, commercial or in private life, is to violate his honour and to discredit his armorial bearings, such acts necessarily affecting

THE FAMILY COAT OF ARMS

Presented to Howard D. Cessna, author of "The House of D'Cessna," in recognition of his efforts and achievements in tracing the Genealogy of our ancient Family—DeCessna, Oct. 29, 1928, by his cousin, Eleanor D'Cessna Van Evera, who searched for years and succeeded in establishing the authenticity of the Armorial Bearings of the family.

also all others who are privileged to bear his family shield. Better not to bear Arms at all than to bear them unworthily.

The obligations should be impressed upon all having right to a Coat of Arms, and they should see to it that no ignoble deed mar the glory of the family ensign. Then will this Heraldic Achievement be a precious possession indeed as it will inspire others to carry into actual practice the highest ideals of life.

To ascertain the full symbolism of the Achievement herein briefly described, it is necessary only to add the signification of its component parts.

LEONARD WILSON.

The Bledsoe Company
Department of Heraldry
San Diego, California

THE COAT OF ARMS
AND ACCESSORIES
OF THE ANCIENT FAMILY OF
DE CESSNA

CONDENSED SYMBOLISM AND EXPLANATION

The *Coat-armour* of this family, as it is described in the ancient record and as emblazoned in the accompanying painting-illumination, is as follows:

Arms: Argent, a double-headed eagle displaying sable, crowned, or, on the breast a circular shield gules charged with a fesse ermine.

Crest: The plume of feathers of an ancient Cavalier.

Motto: "Sine Labe Nota."

Expressed in non-technical terms, this signifies that the shield has a ground of silver on which is superimposed a black double-headed eagle with wings and feet outspread, with a golden crown on its head, and on its breast a red circular shield on which is shown a horizontal band, or fesse, of ermine fur.

Family Coat of Arms

For Crest is borne the ancient plume of feathers of a Cavalier, which adornment antedated the introduction of specific devices for crests.

The *Shield,* or *Escutcheon,* is of Norman shape and dates from the time of Richard, Coeur-de-Lion. There was no part of their armour which the Knights valued more highly than the shield, and none on which they lavished more wealth of decoration. In the Middle Ages it was charged with allusions to the achievements of the bearer, to whose memory it was afterwards consecrated; it was hung over his tomb as a last tribute to his prowess and conspicuous virtues, and it served also an an incentive to others to emulate his worth and valour. The shield symbolized defence and protection.

The *Helmet,* or *Casque,* shown in profile with the visor closed, denotes the rank of an Esquire. It is placed over the shield as its true ornament, it being essentially a real mark of gentility. The helmet is said "to betoken wisdom as well as valour," that of an Esquire signifying particularly "attention, observation and obedience." Helmets, always, should be lined with crimson.

The *Torse,* or *Wreath,* typifies conquest and fortitude. This was a circular roll of silk, intertwined with gold or silver cord, on which the crest rested. Six twists are always shown, beginning with the metal and ending with the tincture of the livery colours, as they appear upon the shield.

The *Crest,* or *Cimier,* has been borne on the helmet of the warrior from the earliest times. The term is derived from the Latin word "crista," signifying "the comb or tuft which grows on the head of a bird." Formerly crests were borne only by those of superior military rank, as such required some distinguishing mark on the battlefield. When seen apart from the Arms the crest denotes the identity of the bearer.

The *Lambrequin,* or *Mantling,* represents the hood or scarf which was attached to the helm and now forms an embellishment to the shield and accessories. It is represented in fanciful twists and turns which are intended to convey the idea that it has been hacked and cut severely in many a well-fought fight.

Each incision is an honourable mark of glory, being evidence of great dangers encountered.

The *Scroll*, or *Riband*, was originally a "gage d'armour," or love-token, and was thence adopted into heraldry. It is usually placed beneath the shield and the motto inscribed thereon, but it is sometimes placed above the crest, and, occasionally, it encircles the escutcheon. The tinctures of the scroll are regulated by those of the Arms.

The *Motto*, or *Devise*, dates from A.D. 1292, and in ancient days, was graven upon the Knight's sword. A motto is not necessarily hereditary but may be discarded and a new one adopted when and as often as desired. A translation of the foregoing motto is "Known without dishonour."

The *Eagle* is the most honourable bearing of all the bird class, of which it is styled the King, and represents extreme courage, strength and nobility of character. "True magnanimity and fortitude of mind is signified by the eagle, which never seeks a battle with small birds or those which, on account of their weakness, are unequal to herself." The little golden coronets on each head indicate eminence.

The *Fesse* is the belt of honour anciently bestowed in recognition of especially meritorious services rendered the country. It signifies that "the bearer must be always in readiness to undergo the business of the public weal." It is formed of two horizontal lines in the centre of the shield.

The *Plume* of Ostrich Feathers is a very ancient bearing, wherein every feather hath pre-eminency "in that it doth bend yet not break."

The metal *Argent*, or *Silver*, symbolizes innocency, cleanliness of character and sincerity of life. The ancients were accustomed to use this metal to denote deeds well performed and worth to be kept in memory. For purposes of illumination, silver is often represented by white; it is of much dignity, and, in the Middle Ages, was preferred to other metals or tinctures because it could be more easily distinguished in the field and seen at a greater distance.

The tincture *Sable*, or *Black*, signifies meditation, solemnity

Family Coat of Arms ⬭

and mourning. It also denotes seriousness of purpose, prudence, constancy, patience under tribulation and sorrow under bereavement.

The *Livery Colours* of this family are: *Cloth*: Dark Drab; *Linings*: Black; *Trimmings*: Black braid and facings; *Buttons and Buckles*: Silver.

COMMENTARY:
Family Coat of Arms

Howard Cessna makes a case that the family Coat of Arms was "discovered" by Mrs. Eleanor Cessna Van Evera at the cost of several hundred dollars. He offers it to all family members as the established emblem of the House of Cessna. There are numerous problems with this assumption.

First let me point out that Cessna, Cissna, Cisne, Sisney, Cesna, Cisney family is not a "House" or "Dynasty" in any form. At best, we are simply a family in exile, and I find that noble enough.

No title or estate exists in France for the descendants of Jean de Cessna to uncover. Titles and estates were granted by the King and the Catholic Church. When given the choice of recanting his faith or forfeiting all his land and title, our ancestor willingly (though bitterly) chose the latter. I think we should honor the courage of his choice, without being jealous for what he abandoned as a matter of conviction.

Secondly is the issue of Heraldry. Coats of Arms were granted to individual knights, and the emblems on they were chosen to represent their family's history, the qualities of their personal character and to commemorate the accomplishments of battle. Land, Title and Heraldry belonged to the individual knight. It might be passed on the his children with permission of the King, but each son would build on the symbols and make his own Coat of Arms.

There have long been numerous companies who purport to research such matters and offer a Coat of Arms which represents a particular family as a whole. Always, for a price which is dear enough to reflect how it will be cherished.

Most experts agree that these are pure speculation. Even when an accurate one is found, remember that it was for a particular individual in our ancestry, not us as a family.

On the cover of this book is a photo I took of the Chateau (Castle) in Menilles, Normadie, France. It was built by Jean le Cesne (also spelled Sesne), about the year 1540. He was the Lord of Menilles and its surrounding regions. It has massive fireplaces at each end of the building. In the fireplace at the north end is a large iron plate bearing a coat of arms, undoubtedly belonging to the current Lord of Menilles.

I am including a photo of that plate on the following pages. Jean's descendants ruled as the Lords of Menilles until the time of the French Revolution. Many of them are buried under the floor of the Chapel next door. However, the names of those buried were chiseled off the stone wall during the Revolution.

I would also remind the reader, that during the French Revolution all nobility were stripped of their titles and lands. This would further negate any hopes of finding any Legacy in France other than Faith and Character.

The Holy See of Antioch (an office of the Catholic Church) offers to search (for a fee) to see if any open titles might be available. Then (for a donation to the Church) you may apply to have that title bestowed on yourself. Remember that such titles bestowed by the Church are not recognized by any civil government and are for social purposes only.

For myself, there is honor enough in knowing how this family overcame great rejection and hardship to become an important part of the fabric of this great nation. The heritage of their stories is a treasure in itself.

Emblem in the back of a fireplace in the Chateau at Menilles, Normandie, France.

CHAPTER III

Tablet to Revolutionary Hero

On Columbus Day, October 12, 1930, the bronze tablet to the memory of Major John Cessna was dedicated with appropriate ceremonies. This Tablet was cemented on a large mountain boulder placed in front of the iron fence enclosing the Major's grave on the farm of Mr. Frank Hemming on Cumberland Road, three miles from Bedford. There is a bronze direction sign on the east side of the public road.

MAJOR JOHN CESSNA
Born January 26, 1726
Died March 31, 1802

CIVIL RECORD

Member Penna. Constitutional Convention 1774. Signed Penna. Constitution 1776. Sheriff of Bedford Co., Penna., 1777-1781. Collector of Excise Bedford County, Penna., 1780. Member of Frontier Safety Committee 1776.

MILITARY RECORD

Joined Gen. Forbes Army with 11 pack horses 1758. Volunteer Soldier at Valley Forge 1777. Field Officer and Member of Board of Court Martial, Valley Forge, 1777.

About two hundred descendants and friends were in attendance at the exercises which were opened with a very beautiful and appropriate prayer by the Rev. E. M. Stevens, a retired Methodist Minister. Mr. Howard Cessna of Rainsburg, a direct descendant of the famous old Major next gave a very interesting speech on the life and times of his noble ancestor.

This was followed by some very entertaining reminiscences by Ex-Governor John M. Reynolds of his friend, another John

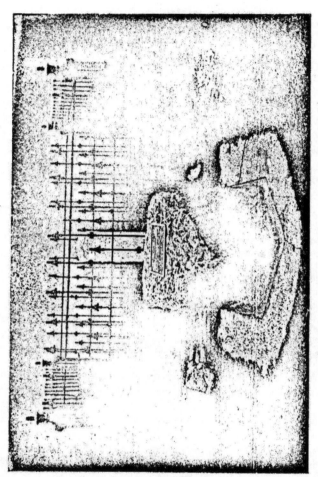

MAJOR JOHN CESSNA TABLET, CUMBERLAND ROAD

Photo of Charles D. and Winona Cissna taken at the marker for Major John Cessna outside Bedford, PA in 1991. Photo was taken by their son, C.W. Cissna.

The House of Cessna

Cessna, who was a noted lawyer and a descendant of Major John Cessna. His remarks showed that the qualities which made the Major great in his day were still alive in his descendants.

Howard Cessna said the appropriate patriotic Prayer just offered by Rev. Stevens was itself a Dedication of this Tablet; that he voiced the sentiment of all descendants present when he extended to the Rev. Mr. Stevens, thanks for having left the bedside of his invalid wife and himself not in robust health, to come out and so agreeably take part.

Howard Cessna on behalf of the hundreds, if not thousands of descendants of Major John Cessna and his brothers, all in the Revolutionary War, thanked Frank A. Hemming and his wife for having deeded in trust to himself and John Cessna Smith, the plot of ground where Major John Cessna is buried.

In the same spirit of appreciation he thanked DeForest Walters of Illinois, whose mother was a Cessna for having some fifteen years past, assisted by Weaver Cessna, erected the Revolutionary Soldiers Monument at the grave. He described how forty years ago Henry Hemming, a descendant, had re-marked the location of this grave saying, that when going to Cumberland Valley with his grandfather, they hitched their horses up at the Public Road and Jonathan Cessna, son of Major John Cessna, said he wanted one more look at his father's grave. Mr. Hemming marked the place but later at the request of Mr. Cessna, he and Weaver Cessna re-marked it, so the exact location is beyond doubt. Cessna wanted the public and especially the descendants to know that the erection of the fence, painting of same, securing mountain boulder, tablet and placing of same was due to the zeal and efforts of John Cessna Smith. All are indebted to him and in this public manner, especially for the absent descendants, he thanked John Cessna Smith.

The Bedford American Legion Post No. 113 then fired a salute over the grave and the Bugler sounded "Taps."

This concluded the exercises. The large gathering from Cumberland, Altoona, Punxsutawney, Bedford and vicinity who had gathered to see the Major's grave properly honored dispersed to their homes.

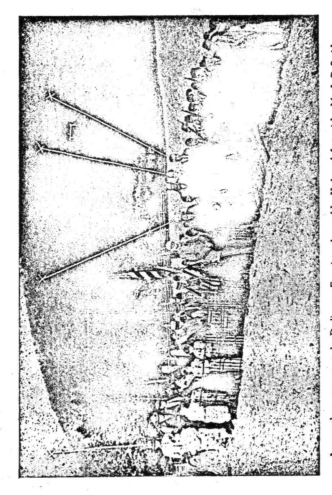

Among those present at the Dedicatory Exercises, denoted by X, from left to right: Mr. J. C. Smith, Hon. John M. Reynolds, Messrs. J. Roy Cessna and Howard Cessna, Esq.

The House of Cessna

No notice of this dedication had been given the Western Cessnas where live ninety per cent of the descendants, owing to the lateness of the season for holding clan meetings; however, some two hundred citizens attended. Included in the crowd were two of the five remaining Civil War Veterans.

Howard Cessna voiced the sentiment of all when he appreciated the coming of Gov. John M. Reynolds to the occasion and lifting his voice of admiration and praise to his old competitor —the late Hon. John Cessna.

A photograph was taken of the gathering and a stenographer was present to record the speeches in detail.

A few of the more prominent points brought out by Mr. Cessna in his speech are as follows:

The Tablet was placed in the spirit that brought forth the existence of the sons and daughters of the Revolution: To perpetuate the name and spirit of those who achieved the American Independence. He stressed the neglect shown by Historians to the Frontiermen but did approve highly the credit by Thomas Montgomery—the author of the Forts of Pennsylvania—when he said there would have been no Declaration of Independence, no United States Government, had it not been for the patriotism and sacrifice of the Frontiermen.

Following are some incidents Mr. Cessna mentioned which pertain to the life or lives of Major John Cessna's relatives:

His father was captured by the Indians near Carlisle in 1756; his grandfather was a Captain in the Battle of the Boyne in 1690.

His brother, Jonathan, built the first house in Louisville, Kentucky, and afterwards was killed while fighting the Indians with Daniel Boone. Later a descendant of this Cessna was called on by the ladies of LaRue County, Kentucky, and asked to donate provisions for Tom and Nancy Lincoln when Lincoln was born.

His brother, Stephen, marched from Bedford to Bunker Hill and was one of the First Riflemen.

A descendant was one of the founders of the State of Nebraska; another started the first live stock exchange in Wyoming; another, James Jackson, was spoken of as a pioneer of Pioneers in the West; was among the first at Sioux City, Omaha, Council Bluff, St. Joseph, and others.

One of his brother descendants manufactured the Cessna Airplane that won the race with thirty-odd competitors from Ocean to Ocean.

In every Military conflict from 1755 to the present time Cessnas did their bit.

Five brothers, descendants of Major John Cessna, followed Gen. Phil Sheridan.

At least fifty descendants from Bedford County and adjoining Counties were in the late World War and counting his brother descendants over the Union in all probability One Thousand were enrolled.

But apparently above and beyond the achievements of any descendant was that obtained by the late Hon. John Cessna.

The poet has sung and rightfully of the praises of men down east like Paul Revere and the historian in like spirit, patriots like Nathan Hale—"but the frontiermen," says Montgomery, "have been neglected."

Descendants of Major John Cessna have just cause to take pride in the fact that in all our frontier history he alone was brought into court and tried for forcibly taking guns from citizens who would not go to war. Remember, thirty-five citizens (Tories) were discovered going to Kittaning to coax the Indians to come scalp and kill their neighbors. Of course at the trial he was acquitted, the authorities in Philadelphia furnishing him with special counsel.

What reading it would make if full details were possible of Indian atrocities in which the Cessnas were connected!

Major John's father was captured in a field near Shippensburg, Pa.—farm now owned by Mr. Bridges—and two of his grandsons killed; a brother, Jonathan, killed by the Indians in Kentucky; a niece, Mrs. Elder, taken captive.

The man whose grave we mark today knew who Capt. Jack

was—the frontierman who devoted the balance of his life to killing Indians after having his loved one scalped.

He knew what Chief was buried on the knob above Rainsburg which town is named after the hunter, Rains. He knew and probably saw Chief Cornstalk who ran along the line of his own men and shot any Indian showing cowardice. He also knew of Chief Wills who was buried on the top of the mountain here overlooking this grave.

Likely he knew Christopher Gist, Washington's guide; also Col. Armstrong, Burd and Crawford; the latter being burned by the Indians while Simon Girty, a white man turned Indian and who never spared any white captive save one, Simon Kenton, stood by.

Howard Cessna in introducing Mr. Reynolds said:

He had heard his uncle John Cessna say he had tried cases for fifty years with men like Thaddeus Stevens, Jeremiah Black, and others but he would just as soon be associated in the trial of a case with John M. Reynolds as any man he ever knew; that Grover Cleveland made no mistake in appointing him Assistant Secretary of Interior, as he was able to fill any Office within the gift of the American people.

Ex-Governor Reynolds said:

I knew the Honorable John Cessna intimately for more than 20 years. He was the son of a Bedford County farmer, and descended from a sturdy race prominent in the affairs of this region long before and since the Revolution. His early education was in the common schools and later at Marshall College, Mercersburg, Pa., where he was graduated in September, 1842, and for the next two years tutored in Latin. He was admitted to the Bedford County Bar in 1845.

At the beginning of his political career, Mr. Cessna was a Democrat. He was Speaker of the Pennsylvania House of Representatives in the session of 1851. In 1856 he was a delegate to the Democratic National Convention at Cincinnati that nominated James Buchanan for the Presidency, and in 1860, was a

THE HONORABLE JOHN CESSNA

member to the Democratic State Convention that nominated Henry O. Foster for Governor, and where the party on his insistence adopted a tariff plank, for the first time, in its platform.

As a delegate to the Charleston Convention in April, 1860, he was Chairman of the Committee on Organization and Rules, and secured adoption of a motion to rescind the "Unit Rule" which resulted in an adjourned convention to Baltimore, and the nomination of Stephen A. Douglas. In 1863 he was again chosen Speaker of the House at Harrisburg, where he ardently aided Governor Curtin in his memorable efforts to marshall the resources of the State in aid of suppressing the Rebellion. About this time Mr. Cessna withdrew his allegiance to the Democratic party, and thereafter was an avowed Republican. He was Chairman of the Republican Convention that nominated General Hartranft for Auditor General in 1865, and Chairman of the State Committee that conducted Hartranft's campaign to victory.

He was a delegate to the Republican National Convention in 1868 that nominated General Grant; also the convention of 1876 that nominated Rutherford B. Hayes, and the convention of 1880, where he supported Grant, declaring ever afterwards, "I am not afraid to say that I was one of the 300 that stood up solidly for Grant." In this campaign he was Chairman of the Republican State Committee, resulting in giving Pennsylvania's Electoral Vote by a large majority, to General Garfield.

Mr. Cessna was a member of the Forty-first and the Forty-third Congresses, and closed his political career by a service as member of the State Legislature in 1893.

For a long period he had been President of the Board of Trustees of Franklin & Marshall College at Lancaster. He attended regularly the services of the Reformed Church at Bedford, and through all his active life was an ardent supporter of the cause of temperance, and an uncompromising foe of the saloon. He was familiarly known as "Uncle John," indicating the kindly feeling of the masses toward him. In the community, in the State and Nation, he was one of the real outstanding men of his time. He set before him a standard of character for his wondrous political and business life which remained unspotted to the end of his career. As an antagonist at the bar, he was a mighty warrior whose keenness of intellect in the presentation of his cause to Judge and Jury made him feared by all who opposed him. His tremendous energy and ceaseless activities in the law and in Governmental affairs wore out a vigorous frame, and he departed this life December 13, 1893, amid the sorrows, alike, of friends and foes.

APPENDIX

With apologies for self-praise I believe I know more of the Cessna History than anyone living. As Uncle John said, it is a pity someone earlier did not take up this work.

In my Book—"The House of Cessnas"—appear some omissions, if not errors and I want, for fear death overtakes me before I am able to correct, to add the following:

Major John Cessna had more brothers than my Book shows and for posterity I wish to state what seems more than probable: Maj. John, Col. Charles and Steven settled here in Bedford County, Pennsylvania. After the Revolutionary War Steven went to Chillicothe, Ohio, and is there buried. Col. Charles according to his descendant, Miss Dorothy Martin, daughter of James Martin of Philadelphia, who had control of all Pullman Cars running east of Chicago, claims he is buried here in Bedford County, Pennsylvania. The Pennsylvania Archives would lead a reader to believe he was indicted for irregularities as an Officer in supplying the Army with provisions. Let all Cessnas dismiss this as a blotch on the name:

1st. In those days criminals were brought to justice. He was never arrested and case not pressed.

2nd. Here on the Frontier an awful conflict existed as to why the Colonial Council and Officers down East did not protect this section as against the Indians, who were being paid twenty-five dollars a scalp for a white man and fifteen dollars for a woman. A tradition handed down through the older Cessnas say his paper money depreciated in value so that gold and silver were required to make a purchase and that feeling like all Frontiermen that here is where provisions were needed, he helped the militia.

From letters published in Pennsylvania Archives his co-patriots, like Daugherty and others, indorse this thought beyond a shadow of doubt.

However, I am in doubt as to whether he lived and died in this County or went down near New Orleans.

As cruel as were the penalties inflicted in those days—ears cut off and thirty-nine lashes for horse stealing—I don't blame him if he did go elsewhere.

Maj. John's brothers, Joseph and William, I take it, went to Muhlenberg County, Kentucky; his brother James went to near Ada, Ohio.

Where his brother Evan settled is only a matter of guess. About twenty years past an Attorney had been examining my land titles for the State and had gone on similar work in one of the Carolinas or Georgia, wrote me he ran across land warrants issued to Cessnas there and I've wondered if some of the older Cessnas did not go into these States.

Further it is to be remembered that Major John's father in all probability had brothers: one, I think, was Stephen as some one by that name took out a warrant for land in Lancaster County, Pennsylvania.

Perhaps it was his descendant who went North around New York and spelled their name Sisney.

Maj. John had three sisters; one married a Brown; one a Mr. Neal; and the other a Mr. Hall.

If, later in life I can go to France I will revise my Book, "The House of Cessna" and make clearer points along the line of ancient Cessnas.

The following is worth including in this appendix as pertains to French History:

From *Extracted Dictionary of the Nobility, 1772, Volume IV, Page 79*: Cisne or Sesne of Minseles in Normandy La Rogue in the History of the House of Harcourt; pages 512, 1316, 1869, 1994, makes mention of one, William Cessna, Chaplin and Secretary of the King of France who had replevin of his temporalities from the King of England, Henry IV—Page 1421, of one Jean Cesne who partook or shared December 26, 1373, a heritage coming from Jean of Bosseyt.

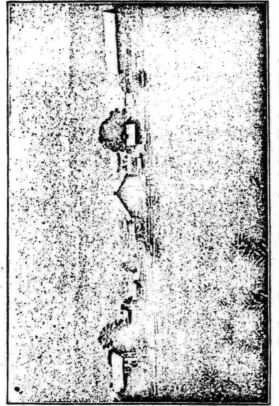

The Cessna Homestead near Rainsburg, Pa., where Maj. John Cessna II lived. This farm has been owned by the Cessnas since 1763.

with grown locust, etc. Mr. Cessna, says he, my education would interest you. I was a little lad and lived on the Smith farm below yours, and it was known that we negros had to quit going to school with the whites.

Well one day three school directors rode up to the school, down at what you call the Double Bricks. Your uncle, Morgart Cessna, was one. He told us all to put up our books and spoke of having colored folks with us and they ought to be educated. The talk continued and finally ended in two voting to expel me while Morgart Cessna voted for me. After the vote, I was ordered to take my books and go home. I took my books and went down to the farm home of Josiah Smith's, and when he saw me coming, he said, "Nim, what does this mean," I said, "I have graduated," we both laughed, but I've been a friend of the Cessnas ever since.

Nimrod was unusually possessed of common sense. He told me many incidents of his day and time. Some really humorous, all concerning the Cessnas or near relatives. Likewise he referred to the underground railroad period in which slave catchers made money capturing run-aways. I hope I've forgotten the name of a negro who betrayed slaves in his care at Bedford and later with this money built a nice home. That home was an eye sore to Nimrod.

COMMENTARY:
The First Generation in America

Howard Cessna quotes Rev. Stapleton's *Memorials to the Huguenots* as evidence that Jean De Cessna came to America in the year 1718. However, Stapleton footnotes that statment by saying it came from Howard Cessna. So they quote each other as proof, and neither can be trusted at this point. There is no record of him on any existing ship manifest. Yet, we should remember that Cessna is not a French name. It is an Americanization, and probably is not the form of the name he would record.

Howard's information came from Congressman John Cessna about 150 years after the fact. But it is a reasonable place to start. In the year 1717 about 5000 Scotch and Irish Protestants from Ireland were recruited by William Penn for his colony. And in 1718 about twice that number, including a large number of Huguenots landed in New Castle. From there they spread out north and west into Pennsylvania.

A puzzle is to why if the family arrived in 1718 are there no references to them owning land or being involved in court records until the 1740's? Family records indicate that several children were born in the 1720's including "Major John" in 1726; but Stephen Sisney serving on a grand jury in 1741 is the first hard reference to the family.

Two possible explanations need to be explored. First is the simple fact that Pennsylvania started in the "Lower Counties" and the earliest records would lie with them. These three counties seceded from the rest of Pennsylvania the same summer as the Declaration of Independence was signed, and formed the State of Delaware. Most of our research has focused on Pennsylvania, and there may be early records in Delaware to help fill in these blanks.

The second explanation is more theoretical and realistic. Most of the people who migrated in 1717 and 1718 came as indentured servants. Wealthy plantation speculators in England funded their passage in exchange for 7 years of service. After 7 years they were free to start building their own wealth and many were given 50 acres of land by the Colony government.

In researching the Richardson side of my family, I learned that John Richardson arrived in Virginia in 1691 as an indentured servant. He worked seven years to pay his passage. Then, he stayed as a hired man with the same plantation owner another seven years to earn enough money to buy his own place. It took several years of working his own land before he had enough cash to record his own deed. His name does not show on any property rolls for nearly 18 years after arriving in America.

It is possible that this was an experience similar to the first generation of our family, and that is why we find no references until 20 years after their arrival. Jean De Cessna may have started life with money and title, but these may not have lasted until 1718.

What records we do find, indicate that there were at least two brothers. Stephen was probably the oldest based on the ages of his children, and John was the younger. Whether or not their father (Count Jean) made the trip is still speculation, but strongly indicated by family tradition.

What follows is a picture of our history, as I have been able to recreate it with what few pieces we have.

Stephen and John Cessna made the trip from Ireland to Pennsylvania about 1718. They were lured by William Penn's promise of a land where they would prosper and live free from the conflict between Catholics and Protestants.

Stephen Cessna appears to be the older brother based on the ages of his children. Each of the brothers appears to have found wives after arriving in America. Stephen's wife was Patience; John's first wife's name is unknown. A reasonable assumption is that it was Rachel, because this is the name given by their son, John Jr (Major John) to his first daughter.

Records indicate that John and his son became a part of Stephen's household. They stayed until John married Agnes 12 years later, and started their own homestead.

Stephen and his younger brother John flourished reasonable well in Lancaster County; carved of land that Penn had bargained from the Indians in 1726. They established "Stephen Sisney's Plantation" and a ferry on Swatara Creek, along the road between Lancaster and Harris' Ferry (Harrisburg).

The ferry was on the main route for transporting trade goods from the Pennsylvania settlements across the Susquehanna River to Indian towns. It stayed busy all year long.

Stephen served on the Lancaster Grand Jury in 1741, and was witness to a number of land deeds in that decade. He purchased the 200 acres that provided him the ferry business on October 17 of 1743.

A petition drafted by him and his neighbors in Middletown, to the county fiscal court, begged for improvement of the road and listed Sisney's Ferry, as one of the landmarks. This road provided their source of prosperity from the heavy trade traffic that moved up and down it. John Sisney also signs the petition and this indicates that Stephen's brother was living with him or at least near him. Stephen's son, John, would have been too young in 1743 to be allowed to sign.

In 1744, Penn purchased land on the west side of the Susquehanna from the Delaware Indians and opened York and Cumberland Counties for settlement. Brother John would take his new wife and move to the town that John Shippen had surveyed in the new county of Cumberland.

Shippensburg would have a brief couple of decades in the sun as a boom town on the edge of the wilderness, and then it faded into obscurity.

Ferry traffic (and thus revenue) dried up when the trade traffic began to cross the Susquehanna River south of Middletown and move their goods through York County to the west. Stephen sold his land and followed the population shift.

He and Patience raised four sons; John, Stephen Jr., Thomas, and Theophilus.

Their son, John married into the Quaker Church, with Pryscilla Foulke in the late 1740's. The sale of the Swatara Creek land yielded enough to stake John to a section of land along Yellow Breeches Creek in the northern end of York County. He provided his neighbors with a ford across that creek on the trade road that led from York to Carlisle.

And Carlisle is where Stephen Cessna moved his family for a "fresh start". He started with a farm just northwest of town. Stephen did not prove to be much of a farmer.

A deep blow to his spirit came in 1751, when his son, John contracted an fever and died in York County, leaving Priscilla and three children; John, Stephen and Ruth. Priscilla would soon marry a Quaker man, Abraham Elliott, and he would move the grandchildren to North Carolina.

Stephen Jr. evidently died without having married and his estate was recorded by his mother at the same time as she settled her husband's estate. The son died a year before his father.

In 1754, Stephen gave up farming and purchased a house in town. He bought lot #187 in Carlisle, near the square. They gave the little farm to their son Thomas who had just married Margaret Gallagher (the proverbial girl-next-door).

Thomas and Margaret became the parents in July of 1755. To ease his father's grief and loss at John's death, the boy was named "Stephen".

In April of 1756, Stephen Cisney and Daniel Hogan fell into dispute over a hat that Stephen had ordered. Whatever his displeasure, Stephen refused to pay and would not (or could not) return the hat.

Debtor laws still being medieval in colonial Pennsylvania, Hogan's law suit caused "Stephen Cessna" to be placed in jail until he would pay.

What happened next became a tug of wills between two prideful men. Hogan had the right to keep him in jail until Cessna would pay for the hat. But Hogan would have to pay the Sheriff for the expense of keeping him in jail.

Cessna could be released the moment he would pay for the hat, or allow anyone else to pay for the hat. He refused both.

These two angry men made a public stand-off of pride and will. It was comical to the community for the first few weeks. But the weeks grew into months, then years. Stephen remained in jail, waiting for his tormentor to yield, and running up the cost of his imprisonment.

In October of 1757, Patience enlisted the help of Arthur Fuller to gain her husband's release because he was so "severely ill" in jail. Her pleas to the court and to Daniel Hogan for mercy, were of no avail.

It seems that Stephen Cessna's lack of social skills had purchased him very little pity from the men of Carlisle. He died there in the Carlisle jail in the winter of 1758.....over the price of a hat.

Patience was left destitute and the home they owned in Carlisle was "Sheriffed" and sold in April of 1758. She moved in with Thomas and Margaret on the small farm, northwest of town.

To make matters even more difficult, the colony was in the midst of a War with the French and their Indian allies. Indian raids were happening all around their farm, throughout the summers of 1757, 1758 and 1759.

Forty miles west in Shippensburg, John Cessna and two of his sons had been kidnapped by Indians in July of 1757. Though they later escaped, it seemed the family had nothing but bad luck to fall its way.

Thomas inherited enough of the father's temperament to get him into serious trouble. Serving in the local militia, he got himself "worked up" during a skirmish with a raiding party.

He made a foolish choice to charge ahead instead of taking cover, and was shot. The wound would fester for several weeks before it took his life. And his death created further hardship.

Patience and Margaret were left alone on the small farm. Theophilus disappeared from the historical record about this time and may well have died in the "Indian Troubles" also. In the 1761 tax roll, the home is recorded simply as belonging to "The Widow Cisney".

On November 30, 1763, Margaret married James Hamilton, an up and coming young lawyer. He had recently arrived from Ireland. She would die trying to birth their firstchild. Hamilton inherited the farm according to marriage laws of the day.

Patience and her grandson Stephen were alone. A grieving widower, Hamilton had little compassion for a mother in law and a step son. He remarried a few years later and became a prominent part of the Carlisle community.

Uncle John however, did not forget the kindness which Patience had offered him after his first wife, Agnes, had died. She had given him a home and been a surrogate mother to his son for nearly a dozen years.

One day in the summer of 1763, Uncle John showed at their door with a wagon to move them to Shippensburg. He helped Patience settle some business first.

The August Orphan's Court docket of Cumberland County records her petition. Patience is asking the court for guardianship of her husband's estate in the amounts that are due her grandchildren. She reports that Stephen and John are minor sons of her son, John who is deceased. These boys have been removed to North Carolina by their step father and mother.

And she reports that Stephen is the minor son of her son Thomas, who is also deceased. William Smith was appointed by the court as the legal guardian of their interests in their grandfather's estate.

Uncle John had suggested hiring an independent attorney, Smith, so as to keep James Hamilton from having too much influence over what little money the family had.

Court records indicate that she is allowed to use the estate for her support, but that it is to go to these three grandsons at her demise. Court records do not mention an inheritance for Theophilus.

Uncle John moved Patience and the boy to his home in Shippensburg. Stephen (his great nephew and namesake of his older brother) became his adopted son on that day. He was 8 years old, the same age as John's son, Evan These two would grow to manhood as close as any twin boys who ever shared the same cradle. This is the Stephen Cissna who fought with the Pennsylvania Rifle Battalion and settled in Chillicothe, Ohio.

John treated him so much like his son, that the family was shocked when John failed to mention Stephen as one of his children in his will, 40 years later.

Stephen and Evans are business partners in Pittsburgh. Stephen married Margaret Hagan, who bought the lot next door to Evans and Mary Cessna, from the Cessna's. Stephen and Margaret purchased another lot in

Pittsburg from Evans as well. And several of Evans' children make the journey to Chillicothe, Ohio with Stephen, Margaret and their children.

I trace the grandchildren of Stephen and Patience Sisney in these two directions. Stephen Cissna, son of Thomas and Margaret, moves to Chillicothe, Ohio and founds that branch of the family. Stephen, John and Ruth, children of John Sisney, are moved to North Carolina by their step father, Abraham Elliott.

This Stephen is arrested with a group of Torries on their way to fight at Moore's Creek Bridge, and imprisoned in Maryland. A petition of his wife for his release records the episode. Stephen's children will move to Kentucky and settle in Muhlenberg County.

1. Lancaster County Court Records: "the first Tuesday in November 1741" Stephen Sesney is sworn and affirmed on a Grand Inquest

2. Quarter Sessions minutes for Lancaster County, PA: November 1744, a petition is made for improving a road between Harris' ferry and Stephen Sisney's plantation at the Pine ford on Swatara. Among 29 petitioners are the names Stephen Cessna and John Cessna.

3. Cumberland County Deed Book: "Stephen Cessna/Sesna, yeoman of Cumberland County and wife Patience make a mortgage to William Dillwood, Carpenter of Carlisle, on 16 March 1754, 20 pounds for lot 187 in Carlisle, due 1 Oct 1754. Lot was originally own by Thomas Porter".

4. Book of John Clum, Sheriff of Cumberland County, PA: 6 Oct 1754. Stephen Cessna vs James Long, papers served.

5. Cumberland County Court Records: April 1756, petition of Stephen Sisney (sick in jail) at the suit of Daniel Hogan, for an unjust debt regarding a hat.

6. Cumberland County Court Indictments: 5 Oct 1757 comes Arthur Foster and Patience Cessna regarding Administration for Stephen Sisney, "being severly sick, in jail regarding payment for a hat."

7. Cumberland County Court Records: 18 April 1758, Property of Stephen Sesna, deceased, sheriffed and sold to William Russell of Carlisle, perry-wig maker.

8. Stephen Sisna, deceased August 31, 1756 in Cumberland County. Goods were not inventories until April 18, 1763. Page 95 of this volume provides the inventory. This is evidently Stephen Jr., son of Stephen and Patience. It is clear he died on August 31, 1756, but the husband of Patience is still alive in Oct 1757. This estate is inventoried and filed in the same court of August 1763 when Patience records Orphan rights for her grandchildren.

CHAPTER V

Archive and Other Records

REVOLUTIONARY MILITARY RECORD

Cessnas—Pa. Arch. V Series

James Cisna—Vol. VI, pp. 58, 136, 590.
Joseph—Vol. IV, p. 394; Vol. 23, p. 308, Capt. of Co.
Stephen—Vol. 23, p. 282; VI 62, 136, 589.
Theopholus—Vol. VI, p. 410.
Theopholus—Vol. VI, p. 386.
Thomas—Vol. IV, p. 282.
Jacob—Vol. VII, p. 535.
James—Vol. VI, p. 404.
Charles Cissinger—Vol. III, p. 560.
Evan—Vol. V, p. 110.
Stephen—Vol. VI, pp. 51, 57.
Thomas—Vol. VI, p. 630.

Pa. Arch. Vol. III 2nd Series, page 274

Judges of the Common Pleas—John Cessna, Sept. 9, 1790; Wm. Proctor, 1790; George Wood, 1790.

Pa. Arch. Vol. II, page 438, 2nd Series, 1747-8

Officers of the Associated Regiment of Lancaster Co., over the river Susquehanna.

John Cessna, ensign.

Pa. Arch. 2nd Series, Vol. I, page 411

Stephen Sisney.

A prisoner taken evidently from British Army and sent to Maryland. Was there a Sisney in the British Army, and if so, was he related to the Cessnas of America?

REVOLUTIONARY SOLDIERS

Cumberland County—V Series, Vol IV, page 281

James Cesna.
Theophilus Cesna, Capt.
William Cesna.
Stephan Cisna.
Thomas Cisna, ensign.
John Cesna—p. 234, Bedford County.
Jonathan Cesna, Jr.—p. 234, Bedford County.
William Cesna—p. 234, Bedford County.
Stephen Cesna—p. 762.
Evan Cesna, Capt.—p. 601.
John Cesna, Jr.
Jonathan Cesna.
Jonathan Cesna, Jr.

Pa. Arch. 3rd Series

John Sensiney, 1736, p. 520.
Stephen Sensiney, 1743, p. 526.
Jacob Sensiney, 1734, p. 518.
Christin Sensiney, 1734, p. 518.
Stephen Cessney, 1743, p. 381.
Warrant for 200 As. in Lancaster County.
Joseph Cessna, 1763, for 300 As. in Cumberland Co., Pa.
Joseph Cisna—Vol 23, 3rd Series, p. 308.
Shown as Captain.

WARRANTS FOR LAND

III Series Vol 25, page 488.

Jonathan Cessna,	400 Acres, 1794—Bedford County
Charles Cessna,	400 Acres, 1794—Bedford County
Stephen Cessna,	400 Acres, 1794—Bedford County
Rebecca Cessna,	400 Acres, 1794—Bedford County
Jonathan Cessna, Jr.,	400 Acres, 1794—Bedford County
John Cessna, Sr.,	400 Acres, 1794—Bedford County
John Cessna, Jr.,	400 Acres, 1794—Bedford County

The House of Cessna

William Cessna,   400 Acres, 1794—Bedford County
Elizabeth Cessna,   400 Acres, 1794—Bedford County

WARRANTS FOR LAND

3rd Series Vol. 25, page 9

Theophilus Cisna, 300 Acres, 1787—Franklin County
William Cisna,   230 Acres, 1787
John Cisna,   24 Acres, 1839—Perry County

3rd Series Vol. 22, p. 320

1784 Cumberland Valley
John Cisna, Esq., 100 Acres
Even Cissna, 150 Acres
Jonathan Cessna 170 Acres
1784 Colerain Township p. 279
Jonathan Cisna
John Cisna, Esq., 200 Acres
1779 Cumberland Valley Township p. 162
Charles Cesna,
Joseph Cesna,
Evan Cesna,
John Cesna, Sr.

INDEX III SERIES PA. ARCH.

	Vol.	Page
Chas. Cessna,	22	162
Evan Cessna,	22	162, 484
Evan Cessna,	23	260
John Cessna,	20	432, 175
John Cessna,	22	162
John Cessna,	23	265
Jonathan Cessna,	22	159, 164
Jonathan Cessna,	23	238, 269
Joseph Cessna,	22	162
Stephen Cessna,	23	258, 273
Stephen Cessna,	22	285

Theopholus Cessna,	20	181, 317
Theopholus Cessna,	23	280
W. Cessna	20	189
John Cessna,	20	452, 603
Theopholus Cessna,	20	597
Wm. Cessna,	20	452, 602
Martin Cessner,	22	14
Charles Cessna	22	8, 69, 87, 154, 263
Charles Cessna,	25	488
Chas. and Thos. Cessna,	24	697
Daniel Cessna,	25	492
Elizabeth Cessna,	25	488
Evan Cessna,	22	8, 69, 87, 154, 263
Jas. Cessna,	23	710
Jas. Cessna	25	490, 491
Jno. and W. Campbell,	24	653
Jno. J. Cessna,		
Jonathan and Joseph	24	651
Joseph Cessna,	22	36, 69, 87
Rebecca Cessna,		
Samuel, Stephen,	23	361, 488
Thomas Cessna,	23	289
Wm. Cessna,	23	752
Stephen Cessna,	24	381

Index to V Series

	Vol.	Page
Chas. Cessna	5	61
Evan Cessna	4	601
James Cessna	4	281, 6, 641
John Cessna	1	24, 4, 234
John, Jr.	6	143, 397
Jonathan Cessna	4	641
Jonathan, Jr.	4	234, 601
Stephen Cessna	4	622
Stephen Cessna	4	212, 762
Thos. Cessna	4	429

The House of Cessna

Thos. Cessna	4	622				
Thos. Cessna	4	622				
William Cessna	4	234, 281,	6,	377,	642,	643
Theopholus Cessna	6	143, 397				
Evan Cessna	5	83, 96, 106				
Chas. Cessna	5	8, 46, 49, 63, 82				
James Cessna	6	96, 396, 422, 433				
John Cessna	5	49, 57, 64, 67				
Jonathan Cessna	5	96, 103				
Stephen Cessna	2	20, 6, 395, 421				
William Cessna	6	369				
William Cessna	6	290				

KILLED AND CAPTURED BY THE INDIANS

Pa. Arch. Vol. III, p. 219—1757

A list of killed and missing at John Cisney's Field.

A list of those killed and missing at John Cisney's Field, about 7 miles from Shippensburg on July 18th, 1757.

Killed John Kirkpatrick, Dennis O'Neidon.

Missing John Cisney and three small boys, two sons of Cisney and one a son of John Kirkpatrick.

These people refused to join with their neighbors who had a Guard appointed them, because they couldn't have their Field reaped the first.

In the History of Shenandoah Co., Va., I find the following: John Cesner p. 227, census of 1785; Jacob Senseny p. 145-276.

COMMENTARY
Can You Explain The Following?

In the next chapter, Howard reports a number of theories and questions raised by family members regarding the occurrence of names like "Cisna" and "Cisena" in Poland and Italy. One theory suggests that maybe the family originated in Italy and came to France. In fact, after the crusades, a number of Italian knights were given land in France.

I have stumbled on a comment by Ernest Nègre which offers another explanation.

"Another significant example can be found in the Norman onomastics: the widespread surname Lecesne,[22] with variant spellings : Le Cesne, Lesène, Lecène and Cesne. It comes from Gallo-Romance *SAXINU "the Saxon" > *saisne* in Old French. These examples cannot be more recent Anglo-Scandinavian toponyms, because in that case they would have been numerous in the Norman regions (pays de Caux, Basse-Seine, North-Cotentin) concerned by these Nordic settlements." (Ernest Nègre, Toponymie générale de la France, Volume II, Librairie Droz. p. 1008)

Normandy is named so for the North men who settled there (Anglos and Saxons). The name Jean le Cesne would mean "John the Saxon". The name Jean de Cesne would mean "John of Saxon (a place or people).

Saxons migrated throughout northern Europe, western Europe and even to the Mediterranean (reaching Poland andItaly). They seized lands, built estates and eventually made alliances with more powerful kings and lords, becoming minor nobility. It is not hard to imagine that "Saxon" would become the last name for some of them.

There is a truly French name which is similar. Le Chesne or Chene means "Oak". However, both Howard and I have received reports from French researchers that Chesne and Cesne/Sesne are completely different names with totally different meanings.

At this point in time, I am convinced that "Le Cesne" or "Le Sesne" would be the original or correct spelling of our family name. I have found references in original French documents which use the spelling interchangeably for the same individuals. In House of Cessna Book III (to be released in 2012) I will report in depth about the frequent appearance of that name in French history.

CHAPTER VI

Can You Explain the Following?

, In my reading Daily papers, etc., I have been like you, struck with the similarity of names coming close to the many different ways in which Cessna is spelled.

The French people originally came from farther East—even Napoleon was an Italian.

It would be wonderfully interesting to know the original history of the real early Cessna in Europe. At any rate, I am including a few items that have impressed me and the exact meaning I will leave to the reader as it is all a guess with me.

The following is taken from the North American during the World War:

TEUTON ALLIES UNABLE TO HOLD MOUNTAIN POSTS—RUS-SIANS MAKE STEADY PROGRESS DESPITE RESISTANCE—BIG STOCK OF MUNITIONS IS CAPTURED AT CISNA.

London, April 5—The attention of the public for the time being is directed toward the great struggle for the Carpathian passes where the Russians apparently are making very steady progress despite the obstinate resistance offered by the Austrian and German troops.

The Russians are on the Hungarian side of both the Dukla and Lupkow passes and with the aid of continual reinforcements are gaining the heights which dominate Uzok Pass.

Even the Austrian official report admits that fighting is now taking place in the Laboreza Valley which is south of Lupkow Pass, while the Russians tonight announce the capture of *Cisna*, an important station on the high mountains between Lupkow and Uzsok Passes, where they captured a great stock of war munitions and provisions.

The House of Cessna

Taken from North American:

MAHANOY PRIEST GUILTY OF ASSAULT—SIX OF HIS PAR-
ISHIONERS ARE ALSO CONVICTED; SENTENCE DEFERRED—TWO
ARE WOMEN.

Pottsville, Pa., May 13—The Rev. Plus *Cesna*, pastor of St. Joseph's Lithuanian Church of Mahanoy City, was convicted in court today of assaulting John Green, sexton of the church. Green testified he was tolling the bell of the church for a funeral when the assault occurred.

Six parishioners of the Rev. *Cesna* who were alleged to have helped him in assailing the sexton, were also convicted, two of them, Mary Petrusky and Mary Yodusky, being women. Sentence was deferred until next week. The fisticuffs in church caused a sensation, particularly when a woman raised cries of "murder."

The jury acquitted Sexton Green of counter charges of assault brought against him by the Rev. Mr. *Casna* and placed the costs on the priest.

Taken from Phila. Inquirer—1933.

DOCTOR 'COOKED TO DEATH' BY NEW REDUCING DRUG.

San Francisco, Aug. 28 (A.P.)—An overdose of a German "reducing" drug was blamed by authorities today for the death of Dr. Hugo *Cessnar*, 40, graduate of the University of Vienna.

The drug containing picric acid, an explosive component, was announced six weeks ago by the Journal of the American Medical Association. Experiments by two young Stanford University medical graduates with animals showed the drug properly administered, should burn away human flesh at about two pounds a week.

Dr. Charles Benninger, Jr., who was attending Dr. *Cessnar* when he died last night, said he virtually was cooked to death, his temperature rising far above normal.

Dr. Benninger said the two experiments were satisfied of the beneficial effects of the drug, but advised that it be taken in small portions over a long period. Dr. *Cessnar* had taken five full grains instead of the grain advised, he said.

Taken from Collier's Encyclopedia Vol. 2, p. 407.

Cesena—a hill town in the province of Forli, Italy, on the Emilian Way.   Among its buildings are: A library founded 1452 by Domenico M. Novello which possesses 4000 precious manuscripts; a Capuchin Church containing one of the best of Guercino's paintings and a noble cathedral.   Productive sulphur mines are in the neighborhood; and the region has been noted ever since Roman times for the excellence of its wines.
Cesena was the birthplace of Pope Pius VI and VII.

In 1357 under Maria Ordelaffi it made a famous defense against Albornoz; in 1377 it was barbariously pillaged by Robert of Genf; on March 30, 1815 Murat gained a victory at this place over the Austrians.   Population about 40,000.

Zanesville, Ohio, April 29, 1922.

Dear Sir: Just received a letter from Greensborough, Greene Co., Ga., in which a Deed states John *Cassna* deeds to David Culberson 400 acres in that County Jan. 1790.   Thought you might want this data.

Letter from my sister Ida—whose husband, Prof. D. C. Stunkard taught or conducted High Schools in Tenn., for many years after being Principal of Bedford, Pa., High School for 14 years.

New Castle, Pa., March 20, 1934.

Dear Brother: In answer to your request would state while in Tenn., I met a lady from Florida who showed me a picture of a boat she saw often in Florida with the name *Cessna*.   It was a very pretty boat such as run on the bay and large rivers.

Ida Stunkard.

CHAPTER VII

John Cessna II Farm

In locating the farm on which John Cessna II, was captured by the Indians, I called on Mr. Stewart, who later wrote me as follows:

June 29, 1927.

Mr. Howard Cessna,
  Lutzville, Bedford County, Pa.

Dear Mr. Cessna: I acknowledge receipt of your kind letter of June 23rd and can assure you that it was a pleasure to meet you, and have a talk with you.   I am sorry, however, that I could not give you more definite information in regard to the old Cessna farm.   Thinking over the matter after you left, I recalled what was spoken of as the "Cessna Farm," when I was a young man.   It was a farm now owned by Christ Long's estate, or the farm adjoining on the East owned by Mr. Robert Bridges, Assistant Editor of Scribner's Magazine of New York.   I have not been able to find out just which one it was, but when I have an opportunity of seeing Mr. Bridges I will have him look the matter up, and will advise you.

I hope that you enjoyed your visit through the Cumberland Valley, and when you get this way again will be glad to have you stop for a longer visit.

With kindest regards to Mrs. Cessna and yourself, I am,

Very truly yours,

Geo. H. Stewart.

Mr. Stewart has since passed on.   He was near 90 years old when I called.   He is the banker of whom it is said owned 100 farms at one time in his section.

Dickinson College, May 10, 1934.

Mr. Cessna: Recently while in York, Pa., I took occasion to hunt for Cessnas in the files but the search brought nothing new to light. I did, however, find that Stephen Cessna was, in 1748, the Executor of the Will of John French of the City of Philadelphia.

John French might have been a family connection.

Respectfully,

Albert H. Gerberich.

Was Stephen Cessna a son of first Cessna to America? If so, he was brother of Maj. John's father.

CHAPTER VIII

Cessnas of Yazoo City, Miss.

Zanesville, Ohio, Aug. 22, 1931.

Mr. J. C. Berryman,
Ashland, Kan.

Dear Mr. Berryman: About a year ago I received a letter from Mrs. Rosa Edmonds residing at the Military Post at New Orleans asking data about Culbertsons and Cessnas. In a second letter she told me she had received a second letter from an old gentleman (a relative) in Yazoo City, Miss., in which he said "My grandfather, Culbertson Cessna, said he came from Kentucky to Miss. His children were: Penelope, Charles, John Culbertson, Sallie, Matilda, Mary Catherine, Margarite, Elizar, Frank Marion, Elizabeth Ann. Culbertson Cessna's wife was Peggy Robinette. Grandfather was born Feb. 19, 1792, married Feb. 28, 1822, died Sept. 23, 1853. My father was Frank Marion Cessna, born Sept. 4, 1837. I (Culbertson Cessna) was born Dec. 29, 1869, at Yazoo City, Miss." I feel certain that these are descendants of Col. Chas. Cessna, but where they lived in Kentucky, I do not know. I told Mrs. Edmonds about Col. Chas. Cessna's court record, etc. I now feel confident that Robert Cessna from whom you are descended was a son of Wm. Cessna (a brother of Col. Chas.) who was one of the early settlers of Muhlenberg County, Kentucky, and who came from Franklin County, Penn'a. With best wishes,

Very truly yours,

L. R. Culbertson.

Likely he was a descendant of Robert Cessna of Kentucky.

CHAPTER IX

Early Court Record and Robert Cessna's Descendants

March 2, 1922.

Dr. L. R. Culbertson,
Zanesville, Ohio.

My Dear Doctor: The following record with dates so far as I have them of the descendants of Robert Cessna and Elizabeth Culbertson.

Robert Cessna D. 1815, M. about 1800 Elizabeth Culbertson.

Issue

(1) Johanna B. 2-2-1803, D. 1-3-1864, M. 9-9-28 Adlai Boyd, B. 1805, D. 1882.

(2) Mary (1) John Smith (2) James Quisenberry.

(3) Margaret D. 1831 (?) or before 1838, M. 10-29-1829 Thos. Newton Berryman.

(4) Sarah Culbertson B. 1808, D. Kickapoo Mission I. Ty. 1846, M. 10-4-1831 Jerome Causin Berryman, B. 2-22-1810, D. 5-6-1906.

(5) Nancy, M. Thos. Kirtley.

(6) Peggy (Elizabeth), M. John Milligan.

(7) Robert John Culbertson B. 4-7-1811, D. 8-27-1900, M. Angeline Calvert, B. 1825, D. 1907.

(8) Charles B. about 1815, D. before 1824.

(1) Johanna Cessna and Adlai Boyd had a number of children, Mrs. Nia B. Schraeder, No. 1824 Deerwood Ave., Louisville, Ky., can give names and information. Adlai Boyd was a prominent and well beloved Cumberland Presbyterian minister in Muhlenberg County, Kentucky, for a number of years.

(2) Do not know where any of descendants of Mary Cessna

and James Quisenberry are, think there were no children by the first marriage. Mrs. Schraeder might be able to advise.

(3) Margaret Cessna and Thomas Newton Berryman, you have this line. Their daughter, Elizabeth, married a cousin of John Beck Culbertson whose son, Romulus Beck Culbertson, is living at Central City, Kentucky, and can give information.

(4) Sarah Cessna and Jerome Causin Berryman had

(a) Gerald Quisenberry Berryman, B. 9-22-1835, D. 1895, M. 6-15-1869 Minerva Anderson Woods B. 9-15-1844, D. 1892.

(b) Emily Green B. 1837, D. 1921, M. about 1867, Giles Russell.

(c) John Wesley B. 1839, Living 1922, M. (1) Laura Matthews, (2) Jennie——, no issue, now residing at Biloxi, Miss.

(d) Elizabeth Cessna B. 1844, D. 1897, M. (1) Warren B. Peck, issue, one daughter Ella M. Charles Shinn, lives in Russellville, Ark. (2) Capt. Fdk. E. Barrow, issue by this marriage, a son Edward, living at Farmington, Mo.

(e) William (died in infancy).

(f) Emily C. (died in infancy).

All their children born at the Kickapoo and Shawnee missions in India Territory (now Kansas) while serving as missionaries from the Methodist Church to the Indian Tribes West of the Missouri River.

(a) Issue of Gerald Quisenberry Berryman and Minerva Anderson Woods.

I. Jerome Woods Berryman, B. Arcadia, Mo. 3-12-1870, M. 6-8-1896 Nancy Annette McNickle at Cortland, Neb. She born Oct. 12, 1871. We have issue Dorothy, B. Elk City, Kans., Sept. 6, 1899 now senior at Washburn College, Topeka; Jerome Charles, B. Ashland, Kans., May 2, 1901, now freshman Centre College, Danville, Ky.; James Wood, B. Ashland, March 2, 1908; Virginia, B. Ashland, 9-15-1910; George Albert, B. Ashland, March 6, 1912.

II. William Stone Berryman, B. Arcadia, Mo. 4-16-1871, M. Kansas City, Mo. 1912, they have Lloyd Price, B. 1914 and Mary Emily, B. 1916.

III. Sarah Chandler Berryman, B. Arcadia, Mo. 9-22-1874, M. Elk City, Kans. 1899 to Wm. Madison Price of El Paso, Tex., now State Senator and a banker resides at Emporia, Kansas. They have Gerald Price, B. El Paso, Tex., 1900, Lloyd Price, B. 1905.

IV. Sartha Emily Berryman, B. May 16, 1876 at Arcadia, Mo., M. 1903 to W. L. Roberts at Ashland, Kans., D. March 14, 1917 (no issue).

(5) Nancy Cessna and Thos. Kirtley. I have no knowledge of this branch or their descendants.

(6) Elizabeth Cessna and John Milligan. I have no knowledge of this line or any of their descendants.

(7) Robert J. C. Cessna and Angeline Calvert. They had a numerous family and have many descendants living in Muhlenberg County, Kentucky, one of which Dr. Jas. Bailey, a prominent physician and ex-service man could give information relative to this line. He resides at Greenville.

(8) Charles Cessna died in childhood and has no descendants.

These are about all the dates and facts I have relative to the descendants of Elizabeth Culbertson and Robert Cessna and I hope they may be of some service in the preparation of the new edition of your geneology.

At any time I can furnish additional information or be of service in connection with the matter, please command me.

Very truly yours,

J. W. Berryman.

February 17, 1931.

Hon. Howard Cessna,
    Bedford, Pa.

Dear Mr. Cessna: I have your recent letter and am glad indeed after the lapse of years to be in touch with you again.

I have had for many years a copy of your book and following its assumption that there were only 4 sons of John Cessna II who lost his life by the Indians near Shippensburg, and all of them appearing improbable as the father of Robt. Cessna, my great grandfather, I had to fall back on Col. Chas. as the only one who could likely have been his father, but that theory too seemed to be disproven through the statement of a Miss Martin of Philadelphia, one of his descendants, who I finally located, so that until I received your letter that John II had other sons I had about come to the conclusion that would never be able to supply the link between Robt. and the rest of the family.

It would seem however that you are right and that your theory was correct.   There is only one thing in the way and that is the apparent rather late marriage of Robt. to Elizabeth Cessna (daughter of Capt. John Culbertson).   I do not know when that was, but as all of their children were born after 1798 apparently he must have married late or have married before in Pennsylvania before he came to Kentucky.   He died in 1815 and his wife in 1826.

Apparently there were two Elizabeth Culbertsons as the wife of Col. Charles was so named but she appears to have been the daughter of Alexander Culbertson of Culbertson Row in Pa., while the other Elizabeth's father, John Culbertson, was likely the brother of Scotch Alexander and the two likely cousins.

There was a Wm. Culbertson in Muhlenberg County, Ky., at the same time as Robert and when the County was organized. This may have been the other son of John II to whom you refer in your letter.   I am enclosing you a chart I have drawn of the family from John of France, if you are correct in your assumption and if you have the time would like to have you look over and OK each item if I have them correct.   Would particularly like to have you, if able, to supply the missing dates as to births and deaths and names of wives of John I and II and of his sons and their wives.

The Wichita Cessnas are quite prominent in the Aviation business of which Wichita is a center.   Clyde Cessna is the inventor of the Cessna Cantilever Wing for a monoplane he builds and this has brought him a good deal of prominence, and his ships are quite noted and very fast.   The death notice I sent you was of his father who has lived for a great many years on a farm in Kingman County.

Very truly yours,

J. W. Berryman.

April 16, 1928.

Mr. Howard Cessna,
Lutzville, Pa.

Dear Mr. Cessna: Your letter of March 8th was duly received but on account of absence and press of other matters have not had an opportunity of sooner making reply to same.

I note you have discovered a Robert Cesna who was cotemporaneous and probably a brother of John II, Charles, Wm., etc. I cannot believe however if this is the case that he could have been my Robert Cessna of Muhlenberg County, Ky. My ancestor Robert Cessna would have been too young, I believe, to have been the one you have discovered for the reason that he must have been a comparatively young man in 1800 which was about the time, or soon after, he was married though he died before 1815.

It will be recalled to you that Col. Charles Cessna was married to Elizabeth Culbertson back before or during the Revolution. Elizabeth Culbertson had a brother Capt. John Culbertson and it was John Culbertsons daughter, also name Elizabeth, who was married to my Robert Cessna. This Elizabeth would have been a niece of the Elizabeth who was married to Col. Charles Cessna.

There was a Wm. Cessna in Muhlenberg County when it was organized and he is mentioned in Rotherts History of Muhlenberg County as having been drawn and serving on the 1st grand jury empanelled. Robert Cessna was also appointed by Gov. Gerrard a justice of the peace for the County when it was organized in 1800.

This is all I have been able to learn and should you get any

The House of Cessna

additional information or light at any time would be glad if you would pass it along to me.

The Culbertson and Cessna families seem to have been brought up or lived in the same locality in Pennsylvania and all of them to have taken an active part in the Revolution and been outstanding citizens as practically every Culbertson and every Cessna old enough to bear arms participated in the War and served in the army and almost every member of either family to have had a commission with rankings from Lieutenant to Colonel in the Pennsylvania forces.

I have often thought if I could find the time that I would like to go back to Pennsylvania and search the records of Lancaster, York, Cumberland and Franklin and Bedford Counties for the records of the two families.

Very truly yours,
J. W. Berryman.

Dr. L. R. Culbertson was looking up family record of J. W. Berryman, Ashland, Kansas, and wrote me as follows:

Zanesville, Ohio, January 19, 1922.

Mr. Howard Cessna,
   Lutzville, Pa.

Dear Sir: I am enclosing two letters which I wrote John M. Reynolds, Esq., of Bedford and which he had just returned me with a statement that he could not look up this date on Bedford County records as he did not have the time and stated that you were familiar with these matters and might be able to give me data and that you formerly were an attorney—I did not know this and therefore see how you are well fitted to look these matters up. I am sending to you the letters I wrote him.

I am also sending you some manuscripts which Mr. J. K. Berryman of Kansas obtained from the Pennsylvania Historical Society. I would like to have you read this and take any notes you wish and return it as soon as possible as I was not authorized by Mr. Berryman to loan it to anybody. I have written on this some data in regard to Surveyor Campbell and what he says about surveying passed Cessna's plantation in 1740. This was no doubt Stephen's plantation at Shippensburg. I notice in the manuscript from Berryman that the first warrant to Stephen Cessna was in 1743 but there is none to John before 1755. It looks to me as though Stephen Cessna Sr. was the father of John Cessna Sr. of Shippensburg.

I was in Chambersburg and Carlisle last summer looking up court records and would have run over to Bedford had I had the time, went on the train, would have liked to have met you.

I will quote you several items I got, in regard to the Cessna's, which you may have. Book 5 page 111 Chambersburg, John Cessna Sr. of Shippensburg to Wm. Cessna of Letterkenny Tp. 100 A. for 100 lbs. in Letterkenny adjoining Samuel Culbertson and others. Deed made 1790—said land was conveyed to John Cessna in 1755.

John Cessna Sr. to Theophilius Cessna 100 A. near Shippensburg for 100 lbs. Book 2 page 287 Wm. Cessna and wife Margaret of Letterkenny to A. Winger land in Letterkenny 650 lbs. Deed made 1790.

This Wm. Cessna son of John Cessna and brother of Col. Chas. Cessna. This Wm. Cessna who went to Muhlenberg County, Kentucky probably after he deeded this land. Although he received a warrant for land in Bedford County I find he did not pay taxes in Bedford County. I am trying to prove whether this Wm. Cessna was the father of Robert Cessna of Muhlenberg County who married Elizabeth Culbertson daughter of Capt. John Culbertson of Kentucky formerly of Culbertson Row and brother of Col. Samuel Culbertson.

In Kentucky, I could find no will or administration of Wm. Cessna and no deeds between him and Robert Cessna to prove their relationship.

Miss Martin's notes of which you have a copy in some respects because of the specific dates in regard to the Cessnas and Culbertsons looked as though they might be authentic yet there is a great discrepancy in her data in regard to Col. Chas. Cessna and his wife Elizabeth because from her data they give no children until 1788 whereas you will notice that Col. Chas. Cessna and Elizabeth Culbertson were married March 4, 1770. It is hardly likely that there would be 18 years before they had any children.

I have found from the data in which a land warrant was issued to Robert Cessna in Kentucky that he probably was born 1775. I could find no marriage record of him in Kentucky but records were not kept there until 1805.

In Carlisle I find a deed John and Agnes Cessna to R. Urie for land in Pennsboro Tp. in 1768. I found also Stephen Cessna letter of administration issued to his administrators Arthur Foster and Patience Cessna Oct. 5, 1757—no account filed. I presume this was the Stephan Cessna Sr. Orphans Court 1762, Patience Cessna came to court and asked for guardians during minority for Stephen and John, two minor sons of John Cessna deceased and Stephen Cessna son to Thomas Cessna during minority. Wm. Smith was appointed guardian.

At Chambersburg, Theophilius Cessna and Sarah his wife of Fannett Tp. land in Southampton Tp. to John Breckenridge land conveyed to him by John Cessna. John Cessna received warrant for same 1755. Date of deed 1795.

I send you this data for your presual, also will make a request that if you have the time and care to do so, I would like to have you go to the court house at Bedford and look up data which I requested of John M. Reynolds to look up. Also the deeds which I mentioned in second letter to Reynolds in regard to John Culbertson. Also deed of James Culbertson about 1778 to 1785. Mr. Berryman said he would pay for having this data looked up and as you are an attorney and understand this work if you have the time and inclination, you would be the best party to look it up; if you can not do it would you please give me the name of some good lawyer in Bedford or would you ask some lawyer if he would do this and put him in communication with me and if he will do this turn this data over to him, excepting the data belonging to Berryman—do not let that out of your hands.

Very truly,

L. R. Culbertson.

P. S.: I wrote Allegheny, Washington, Westmoreland, Blair, Huntington, Perry and Fulton and Bedford County, Pennsylvania court officials *in re*. Chas. and Elizabeth Cessna and they said they could find nothing, likewise from Montgomery and Miami Counties, Ohio.

Dr. L. R. Culbertson,
   Zanesville, Ohio.

Dear Sir: Having just returned from Louisville, Kentucky, my brother James Martin has given me your letter in regard to Col. Charles Cessna and his wife Elizabeth Culbertson.

John Cessna; born north of Ireland 1679 or 1680; died 1751; immigrated 1709; married Priscella Foulke 1717. Issue: John Cessna II; born January 20, 1718, Lancaster County, Pa.; died September 30, 1796, Cumberland County, Pa; married April 4, 1740, Cumberland County, Pa., Sara Rose born Feb. 6, 1720 in Lancaster County, Pa. and died July 1, 1792 in Cumberland County, Pa. Issue: Col. Charles Cessna; born March 2, 1744, Cumberland County, Pa.; died July 30, 1837, Bedford County, Pa.; married Elizabeth Culbertson in Cumberland County, Pa. March 4, 1774 who was born Jan. 31, 1747 in Cumberland County, Pa. and died Aug. 19, 1831 Bedford County, Pa. She was the daughter of Captain Alexander Culbertson, born May 17, 1714, Antrim County, Ireland, died April 2, 1756, Cumberland County, Pa. and Mary Duncan who were married November 4, 1740. She was born March 14, 1725 Lancaster County, Pa. and died August 3, 1794, Franklin County, Pa.

Col. Charles Cessna, Major of the 2nd Battalion Bedford County Militia. Col. George Wood, commanding July 1776, Lieutenant Colonel of the 1st Battalion Bedford County Militia. Col. Parker, commanding December 1777 was also Lieutenant Col. commanding 1st Battalion Bedford County Militia 1781. Printed authority Vol. 14, 2nd series Penn. Archives, pages 642, 644, 657. Issue of Col. Charles Cessna and Elizabeth Culbertson. James born 1788; died same year. William Franklin born 1790; died same year. Rachiel born November 30, 1793,

Bedford County, Pa.; died May 6, 1877; married Samuel Mc-
Causlin II; Rebecca born 1797; married John Husband; Maria
born 1800; married James Jones; Mary Ann born 1802; died
single.

I am descended from Rachiel who married Samuel McCauslin II. Their daughter Mary McCauslin Martin was my grandmother. I am a daughter of the American Revolution, through
Col. Charles Cessna and my father was a member of the Society
of Colonial Wars, through Captain Alexander Culbertson.

There are a number of Culbertsons in Louisville, Kentucky;
Samuel Culbertson who married Miss Louise Craig. They have
two sons, William and Craig. Mr. Samuel Culbertson lives 4th
Street near Burnett, Louisville, Kentucky. His wife is a friend
of my mother who was Lula Hays of Louisville.

I hope this will be satisfactory.

Very sincerely,

July 10, 1921   Dorothy Helen Martin.

August 29, 1921

Dear Mr. Berryman:

I have been to Chambersburg, Carlisle, West Chester and
Media and looked over court Records for Culbertsons and
Cessnas and got stacks of information. Met John N. Culbert-
son at Chambersburg and visited Row, Rocky, Spring, Va. At
Chambersburg I found as follows *in re.* Cessnas: Deed Book 5,
P. 11 John Cessna (or Cisney) grantor of Shippensburg to Wm.
Cessna of Letterkenny Tp. Franklin County, Pa. conveys 100 A.
for 100 pounds in Letterkenny adjoining land of Samuel Cul-
bertson and others made 1790. John Cessna Sr. to Theophilus
Cissna 100 A. near Shippensburg for 100 pounds.

Vol. 2, P. 287, Wm. Cessna of Letterkenny Tp. and Margaret his wife to a Winger land in Letterkenny for 650 pounds.
Said land conveyed to John Cessna Feb. 26, 1755. Made deed
1790. (This must have been date Wm. Cessna went to Ky.)

Book 12, P. 764. Robert Cessna admr. Margaret Cessna of
Fairfield County, Ohio, deed who was one of the heirs of John

Maguire and wife for $31 paid me by John Maguire give quit claim. Made 1821 (Your ancestor died 1817 so this is not your party).

Carlisle deeds: Book C. 261. John and Agnes Chessner to R. Urie land in Pennsboro Tp. in 1768. John Cisner of Hardin County, Ohio, August 1, '43, administration, no account filed. Stephen Cessna letters of administration to Arthur Foster and Patience Cessna October 5, 1757 (See A. 22) No account filed. (Patience may have been mother or sister of above).

In 1762 Patience Cisney came into court and asks for guardians during the minority for Stephen and John, two minor sons of John Cisney, deceased and Stephen son of Thos. Cisney during their minority and court appoints Wm. Smith Esq. guardian of said Stephen, John and Stephen Cisney. (This would show there were other sons i. e. Thomas. Deeds show Wm. was a son but of age in 1762).

Deed Book 3, P. 429. Made deed 1793. John Cessna Sr. of Shippensburg for 100 pounds deeds to Theophilus Cessna of Southampton Tp. land in Southampton Tp. (no wife given in deed) (Must have been my John who went to Bedford).

Vol. 3, 120. Theophilus Cessna (or Cisney) of Fannett Tp. and Sarah his wife land in Southampton to John Brackenridge. Land conveyed to him by John Cisney in 1793. John Cessna received warrant for same in 1755. Made 1795. You are not descended from Irish Samuel Culbertson by his son John of Westmoreland County.

The last deed I can find of John Culbertson, brother of Col. Samuel and son of Irish Capt. Alexander, was in 1781 when he and his brothers quit claimed. He had no wife at that date as no wife signed. His residence at that date was Lurgan Tp. (Row) and Elizabeth and Charles Cessna, Bedford County. I feel sure now he went to Kentucky at that date and was Capt. John your ancestor John son of Irish Samuel and wife Margaret sold his farm in Row in 1786 and moved to Westmoreland County, Pa. Died 1797.

I heard from Blair, Huntington, Bedford, Westmoreland and Allegheny County, Pa. and Chas. and Elizabeth Cessna not found on records (will or admr). Not at Carlisle or Chambersburg. The State Librarian at Frankfort, Ky. looked over a lot of dates, D. A. R. records and County Histories, she says that Rothert's history of Muhlenberg says among the first grand jurors in 1799 were John Culbertson and Wm. Cessna. First Justice of Peace, Robert Cessna. So you see we have located Wm. Cessna in Pennsylvania and in Kentucky. I feel sure this was Robert's father and he must have been born about 1741. He was in Revolution in Col. Samuel Culbertson Regiment. The State Librarian, Kentucky, gave me Samuel, John and James with Virginia military records and I have written to Richmond for these. County Clerk of Court at Hartford, Lexington and Lincoln County, Kentucky and Louisville say there is nothing on records. I wrote Librarian at Frankfort to pursue investigations further in County histories of earliest counties. I will write Logan County and several other counties for court records of Cessnas and Culbertsons. Land office at Frankfort has the land warrants which I will get on my return home. Col. La Bree of Louisville has nothing. He has a copy of will, inventory and accounts of Irish Samuel of Row which same Culbertson gave him years ago for which he wants $35.00 but as you are not descended from Samuel they would be of no interest to you. With best wishes,

Very truly yours,

L. R. Culbertson.

P. S. Please send copies of this letter to Howard Cessna of Lutzville and to Robert Culbertson in Kentucky.

Through the courtesy of Miss Dorothy Martin, descendant of Col. Chas. Cessna, I obtained the following:

The earliest known ancestor of the family of the name of Cessna, came to America, according to tradition, about 1718-20 and settled in the eastern part of Pennsylvania. He was a Huguenot from the South of France, who settled and married in Ireland after the Battle of the Boyne in which he participated.

Some authorities state that this original ancestors Christian name was Joh, and that he came to America in 1690 (History of Bedford, Somerset and Fulton Counties, Pa., P. 354, 428) but the archives and other records do not show any one of the surname of Cessna in Pennsylvania prior to 1743, when Stephen Cessna, on October 17 of that year, as Stephen Cessnay or Sisseney, warranted a tract of land situated in Lancaster County:

Stephen Cessnay, 200 A. Oct. 17, 1743, Lancaster County, Pa. Ar. 3rd series, vol. XXIV, p. 381.

Stephen Sissenay, 200 A. Oct. 17, 1743, Lancaster County, Do., p. 526.

Lancaster County at this date, 1743, included all land that at present lies, not only within the present limits of Lancaster County, but all that territory lying west of the Susquehanna River, (south of the Juniata) as far as civilization extended. In 1750, Cumberland County was carved out of Lancaster and 1771, Bedford was organized out of Cumberland.

The Scotch Irish emigration began to come to Pennsylvania in very large numbers in 1718, settling for the most part in what was then Chester County in that part which in 1729 was incorporated into the newly erected Lancaster County. It would therefore seem quite probable that the emigrant ancestor came to Pennsylvania with these pioneers, Scotch Irish Presbyterians, while these pioneers practically all possessed themselves of farms, it was not until a later period, that, in order to secure their property rights to their improvements, they were encouraged to make application to the Land Office of the Commonwealth, and receive patents to their lands. Hence the indications are that Stephen was the name of the original ancestor and not John. This could only be determined by an examination of records at the Land Office at Harrisburg, and records at Chester, Lancaster and Carlisle.

The first authentic record of the family which we find are two warrants issued to John Cessna who was said to be the son of the emigrant. John Cessna was born in Ireland in 1718 and was brought to Pennsylvania by his father, while still an infant

The House of Cessna

(Pennsylvania Historical Magazine, Vol. III, p. 199). September 18, 1755 John Sisney made application for a tract of 25 A. of land in Cumberland County and December following acquired an additional 100 A. in same.

John Sisney 25 A. Sept. 8, 1755, Cumberland County.
John Sisney, 100 A. December 16, 1755, Cumberland County, Pa. Ar. 3rd series, vol. XIV, p. 756.

This is the first appearance of John Cessna's name on the State records. On June 3, 1762 John Chisney received a patent for 150 A. also in Cumberland County.
John Chisney, June 3, 1762, Cumberland County, Do., p. 650.
On May 17, 1763 Jonathan and Joseph Cessna were granted 300 A. by the Commonwealth, which was also in Cumberland County.
Jonathan and Joseph Cesnay, 300 A. May 17, 1763, Cumberland County, page 651.
While on June 3, the same year Charles Chisney was granted 100 A. in same county.
Charles Chisney, 100 A. June 1, 1763, Cumberland County, p. 651.
Jonathan, Joseph and Charles all being sons of the above named John Cessna. On August 2, 1766, John Cisney on behalf of his son Charles Cisney entered a caveat against John Busen being granted a tract of 47 A. of land, claiming that these same 47 acres were part of Charles Cessna's precious patent:

Caveat Book No. 3. Aug. 2, 1766.
John Cisney at the request and on the behalf of his son Charles Cissney enters a caveat against accepting a survey made by John Owens on Forty Seven Acres of land on Juniata River, Cumberland County, or any other patent issuing thereon, he the said Charles Cisney having a prior warrant for the said land. The last Monday in October is appointed for a hearing.
James Tilgeman, Sect'y. Pa. Ar. 3rd series, vol. 11, p. 355.

However on August 24 following they withdrew their objections, as the matter was arranged satisfactorily out of court:

John and Charles Cesnay Agt.; John Owens—on caveat.

The plaintiffs appear and inform the Board that the matter is agreed and they withdrew their Caveat.

At a meeting of the Governors on Monday 25th of August, 1766 Minutes of the Board of Property.

Do.   Vol 1, p. 151.

Another entry in the Caveat Book shows that the land granted to Joseph Cessna incroached upon that of Christian Eversole. Before the long contested boundary line between Pennsylvania and Maryland was finally settled, the patents issued by the two colonies often overlapped and great trouble arose which often led to bloodshed:

Caveat Book No. 4.   Land Office March 17, 1768.

Christian Eversole enters a Caveat against the accertance of a survey for Joseph Cessna on a tract of land near Rome Creek, which leads into Evett's creek in County of Cumberland alleging he hath a Maryland patent for the same.

Do.   P. 425.

On Sept. 4, 1767 John Cessna took up another tract of land in partnership with William Campbell. This also lay in Cumberland County.

John Cessna and William Campbell, 200 A. Sept. 4, 1767, Cumberland County, Pa. Ar. 3rd series, vol. XXIV, p. 653.

John Cessna lived and died within the present limits of Cumberland County. His will under date of 1793, is recorded at Carlisle and in it he calls himself as of Shippensburg, which is in the extreme western part of Cumberland County, near the Franklin County boundary line.

Will of John Cessna, Shippensburg, Pa., dated Oct. 24, 1793. Proved Oct. 13, 1796, names his sons, John, Charles, Joseph, Jonathan, deceased; Evan, William; eldest daughter, Mary Neale, deceased; daughter, Elizabeth Jones; daughter, Margaret Hall; youngest son, Theophilas; James.

Mentions land in Southampton Township conveyed from

The House of Cessna

William Campbell; land on Juniata Creek above Jack's Narrows; Island in Juniata River; land where Prigmore's land now is; land from Mr. Blunston, in York Co.; land taken up with Messrs Fulton and Wallace; land adjoining place formerly Robert Gabey and Samuel Culbertson. Bequeathes to Elizabeth, minor daughter of son Willis. Executor, son James.

Will Book F. p. 40, 41. Carlisle, Pa., Cumberland county, Will Abstracts. Mss Copy in Poss. Gen. Soc. Pa.

Nearly all of the sons of John Cessna settled permanently without the limits of Cumberland County. John, Jr., Charles, Joseph, Jonathan and Evan located in what is now Bedford County. Theophilas and William in what is now Franklin County. Of James no further record. He may have remained in Cumberland County.

BEDFORD COUNTY WARRANTIES

Charles Cist	300 A. May 12, 1773
John Cessna	400 A. Apr. 10, 1794
Joseph Cessna	400 A. Apr. 10, 1794
William Cessna	400 A. Apr. 10, 1794
Jonathan Cessna	400 A. June 21, 1794
Charles Cessna	400 A. June 21, 1794
Stephen Cessna	400 A. June 21, 1794
Rebecca Cessna	400 A. June 21, 1794
Jonathan Cessna Jr.	400 A. June 21, 1794
John, Sr. Cessna	400 A. June 21, 1794
John Jr. Cessna	400 A. June 21, 1794
William Cessna	400 A. Aug. 15, 1794
Elizabeth Cessna	400 A. Aug. 15, 1794

The several tracts taken up by the Cessna brothers lay in what was and still is Coleraine and Brother's Valley Townships, Bedford County. Bedford was made into a separate County in 1771, being created out of the most Western part. Coleraine was one of the original townships and comprised, in 1771 a large part of the south eastern part of the new county. It is situated wholly within the Valley long known as Friends Cove, which lies between Evits and Tussey Mountains, and was named for John Friend, who secured a title to this large tract in 1762, patented to by the name of "Friends Cove." Contemporaneous with Friend, came the Cessna family into the Cove, who also took up a large tract in the vicinity, a part of which land has descended through successive generations of the same family to the present day.

TAXABLES CUMBERLAND VALLEY TWP., BEDFORD CO., PA.

1773	Charles Cessna	297 A.
1773	Joseph Cessna	250 A.
1774	Evan Cessna	200 A.
1774	John, Sr. Cessna	100 A.
1775	Charles Cessna	
1776	Charles Cessna	
1776	Evan Cessna	
1776	John Cessna	
1776	Robert Culbertson	
1783	John Cessna, Esq.	100 A.
1783	Charles Cessna	400 A.
1783	Jonathan Cessna	170 A.
1783	Evan Cessna	150 A.
1783	John Cisney, Sr.*	100 A.

* Non-resident

In 1791, Stephen Cessna was in Pitt Township (Pittsburgh) Allegheny County.

During the Revolutionary period, Bedford comprised Bedford, Fulton, Somerset, Huntingdon, Blair, and Cambria Counties. Among those who immediately became identified with the struggle were: Major John Cessna, Col. Chas. Cessna. (History Bedford County, Pa., p. 81, 428).

Foremost among the Cessna brothers was John, eldest son of John Cessna, Sr. of Cumberland County. John Cessna serves as an ensign in the Provincial Service, 1747 as did also his brother Charles. Upon the organization of Bedford Co. 1771 John Cessna headed the list of Provincial Magistrates. He was a member of the Convention which framed the Constitution of 1776; served three years as sheriff of the new county, 1777-81-83; Major of Bedford County Militia Troops during Revolutionary War; and Justice of the Peace, 1779-82-90. Mr. Cessna died about 1802. He raised a large family of children and his numerous descendants are scattered over the western and southern states. Among these was John Cessna, Esq. a prominent member of Congress, 1899. (Pennsylvania Historical Magazine, vol. 111, p. 199).

Among those who secured patents for land in Bedford County was a Stephen Cessna. In 1790 we find one of that name in Teboine Township, now in Perry County, and 1791, the name appears as a taxable in Pitt Township, Allegheny County; in 1794, was one of those who took up 400 A. in Bedford County.

The will of John Cessna, Junior, of Bedford dated 1802, names wife Elizabeth and the following children: Charles, Evan, James, Henry, Sarah Rose; executors, Jonathan Cessna II. Egles notes and queries, 1899, p. 209.

Charles Cessna, son of John Cessna, Senior of Cumberland County, Pa. was early identified with the Military and Civil history of the county. He served in the Revolutionary War, 1776, as Major of the 2nd Battalion of Bedford Militia in 1777 as Lieut. Col. of the 1st Battalion, and 1781 as Lieut. Col., of same the company being designated as of Coleraine Township etc., in 1780 is commissioner of Purchase, in same list Robert Culbertson appears as Sub-Lieut. of the County and again in the list of General Officers in Pennsylvania Militia, of Bedford County, we find among the purchasers and Place of Delivery, Charles Cessna, Bedford, Bedford.

Charles Cessna married Elizabeth, daughter of Captain Alexander Culbertson, of Culbertson Row, Franklin County, Pa. and daughter of the Robert Culbertson mentioned in Bedford County records. When Bedford County was organized 1771, among the first Grand Jurors names were: Charles Cessna, Robert Culbertson. Like his brother John Cessna, Charles soon became active in the civil life of the county. In October Charles

Cessna was elected to the General Assembly as representative of Bedford County.

This indenture made the 14th day of October 1777, between Thomas Urie, Esq., High Sheriff and Robert Culbertson, John Moore, assistant Judges, witnesseth the in pursuance of the laws of the State of Pennsylvania 14th day of October at Bedford County, Herman Husbands, Charles Cessna, William McComb, etc., were duly elected representatives from County of Bedford to sit in the General Assembly of the State the ensuing year.

Thomas Urie, Robert Culbertson, Evan Cessna, Samuel Moore. Pa. Ar. 6th series, vol. IX, p. 14.

In January and October 1779 Charles Cessna was elected commissioner of Supplies, which office he held for a number of years. Oct. 7, 1780 he and Samuel Moore offered themselves as security for John Cessna, Esq. as High sheriff of the County.

Bedford County Oct. 7, 1780. We the undersigned subscribers do offer ourselves as Security for John Cessna, Esq. High Sheriff of Bedford County for the ensuing year. Witness our hand and seal. Charles Cessna, Samuel Moore. Pa. Ar. 6th series, vol. XI, p. 19.

In 1781 he was again elected as Representative to the Assembly and the same year John Cessna being again elected Sheriff offers his brother as security.

A return of General Election of the County of Bedford was received and read by which it appears the following gentlemen were duly elected to wit. Representatives, Bernard Dougherty, Charles Cessna; Sheriff, John Cessna.

John Cessna Esq. Sheriff elect for Bedford County now offers Charles Cessna and Allen Rose of said county as sureties for the faithful performance of the duties of his office.—Colonial Records, vol. XIII, p. 134.

Still again on October 12, 1782, John and Charles Cessna act as Bondsmen:

We the Subscribers do offer ourselves as surety for Abraham Miley for the true performance of the Sheriff Office of Bedford County. As witness our hand this 12th day of October, 1782.

John Cissna, Charles Cissna. Pa. Ar. 6th series, vol. XI, p. 22.

At a meeting of the Council, Philadelphia, the following order was drawn on the Treasurer:

In Council. Phila., Wednesday, June 5, 1782. In favor of Charles Cessna, Esq., for the sum of 100 pounds State money the 7th day of April, 1781, being extra allowance for his services as commissioner of Purchase in the County of Bedford.

In favor of Charles Cessna for the sum of 100 pounds Specie to be delivered by him to Messrs. Cessna and Dougherty, contractors, for supplying with provisions the Ranging Companies of Militia in actual service in the County of Bedford for which the said contractors as to account.—Col. Records, vol. XIII, p. 298, 99.

November 23, 1782, by a vote of the Assembly, it was ordered that the Comptroller General, John Nicholson, should call upon all officers of the Government who have received public money and have not accounted for same and to call for immediate settlement of same.—Votes of Assembly, 1782, p. 751.

The Council met. Phila., Thursday, Sept. 11, 1783. Resolved that the Attorney General be directed to institute action against Charles Cessna, Bedford County, late member of the House for forgery and perjury.—Col. Rec. vol. XIII, p. 684.

The Council met. Phila., Tuesday, Feb. 3, 1784. Mr. Rush, Mr. McClay and Mr. Clymer, a committee of the house attending in Council, a conference was held upon the subject of a letter from Thomas Smith Esq., to the Comptroller General, on the case of Charles Cessna's sureties and accounts.—Col. Rec., vol. XIV, p. 29.

Council met. Phila., Monday, Nov. 29, 1784. An order was drawn upon the Treasurer in favor of George Campbell Esq., for six pounds and fifteen shillings, to be paid to Robert Galbraith and James Hamilton, being the fees allowed to them for engaging in the cause depending between the Commonwealth and the Sureties of Charles Cessna, late of Bedford County and the expense of a writ of Certiorari, according to the Comptrollers report.—Col. Rec., vol. XIV, p. 266.

Among a number of old Supreme Court papers in the possession of the Genealogical Society we find in lists of cases continued from time to time that this case was still pending or rather those held over in 1790 and still in 1807.

Pa. Arch. vol. 9, p. 236.   Capt. Chas. Cessna to Col. James Morgan, 1781.

Bedford, June 30, 1781

Sir: The Bearer Mr. Isaac Worrell one of my Deputies in the purchasing way in this County goes to you for the express purpose of getting your advice in order to direct and govern me in the Departments, the distress of this County is truly great, murders and depredations are committed almost every week, and not a single article can be had for the money that's now current; I am even threatened and inveighed against by the people, for not having suitable provisions for such as Military duty, and it is impossible for me to get it for the money I have; I am indebted to numbers in consequence of such articles as we purchased and so are my Deputies, having engaged on the credit of the money and which is now useless; and unless something be done in order to enable us to get provisions for such as are employed to protect the county, I am afraid the settlement broke up totally and that very soon.   It is impossible for me to send you an accurate return having purchased on the credit of the money which was in so fluctuating a state while it dubiously passed as to leave no room for a certain price in any article; and now no person would receive any quantity of it for a single beef cattle.   I beg you will dispatch the bearer with all due haste and I hope in such a manner equipped as will enable me and those that are employed by me in the service to do the requisite and necessary duty expected of us.   I am sir, with great respect.

Your most obedient H'ble Serv't,

Charles Cessna, Capt.

CHAPTER X

James Cessna, Brother of Maj. John Cessna; His Will; His Father's Will and Names of Descendants

This James Cisna was a brother of Maj. John, and I give this letter to show scores of similar ones received. James was in the Revolutionary War, Vol. VI, Pa. Arch. p. 404. Buried at Shippensburg, and grave recently marked by D. A. R's.

Columbus, Ohio, Sept. 21, 1928

Mr. Howard Cessna,
Bedford, Pa.

My dear Mr. Cessna: I am writing you in behalf of the book you had published about eighteen years ago, called the House of Cessna. My name is the same and as our line is not completely followed up in that book, I can tell you the reason and have some information concerning this branch that will perhaps help us find the broken link.

I am very anxious to find this link in our family history for several reasons: I should appreciate it very much if you could give me the clue.

When the information was asked for at the time the book was published, the person with the most information was not reached and this information I have is in the hands now of Clarence Cessna, an attorney in Kinton, Ohio, and a second cousin of mine. His father had the Bible records and also a mill and land deed of my ancestors. My father was William Manley Cessna, son of John Davis Cessna, son of William Cessna, who came from Shippensburg, Cumberland County, Pennsylvania. He bought land in Hardin County, Ohio, in 1835, and settled there to live and died and is buried in Salem Cemetery, Hardin Co., Ohio. His father was James Cisna, Southampton Township, Cumberland County, Pennsylvania. I have a copy of his last will, which states it was written and with a codicil a year later, registered in Carlisle, Cumberland Co., Pa., in 1832, April 15th. He mentions in his will, seven children, James, John, William, Elizabeth, May, Margaret, and Sarah. Now I put in the details so that if you have information concerning this family you could easily discovered it. Would it be possible for you to give me any information as to the father of James (Cessna) Cisna, Southampton Township, Cumberland Co., or could you tell me how I might gather the records. As you have already traced the families of this name so well in the book, I venture to ask this favor that I may see where this connection is a part of John I, in the book of Cessnas.

Thanking you very much for whatever you can tell me, I am sincerely,

Mary Cessna,

60 S. 3rd St., Columbus, Ohio.

John Cefsna was born in the year 1692, and died about the year 1798.

This John was born in Ireland, and the first that came to America. His father was a Frenchman.

John Cefsna Bible bought 1791.

Johnathan Cefsna was born April the first day, 1789.

Johnathan Cefsna book bought in 1820. This book was my great grandfather's of Shippensburg, Pennsylvania, who lived to the age of one hundred and seven years.

—Copied from Old Bible.

March 13, 1932

Mr. Howard Cessna: Since I have re-read Mrs. Prices letter I believe it best to copy the entire letter, as then you will be more apt to not be confused, so it follows in full:

"Forest, Ohio, June 18, 1931

Dear Cousin: I am happy to tell you that I located the record which Howard Cessna tried so hard to secure at the time he was getting out the book "House of Cessna," about thirty years ago.

The House of Cessna

At that time he had written to my grandfather, who lived in Ada, Ohio, and asked for some reliable data, which would connect our branch of the Cessna family with the early French Cessna ancestry.

My grandfather was ill at the time, and seemed unable to get the desired record copied, due perhaps to his illness. I was little more than a child at the time and I remember how disappointed my father was that our branch of the family was not more clearly connected with the early John I of France. However better late than never, I am sending you a copy of what was written in an old Bible, in ink, but part of it only discernable with a magnifying glass. But I am satisfied it is correct and I shall also send a copy of it to Howard Cessna since I have had a recent copy of the booklet, concerning the bronze tablet, and I wish to thank Howard Cessna for it.

I secured a copy of the House of Cessna from him about five years ago and at that time, I could not secure this record as the person in whose possession it was, lived in the state of Iowa. Howard had written that he hoped to have a new edition of the book printed with many corrections and much more definite data. I am glad you wrote to me about it, as it brought it to me more clearly that I had neglected to do, what I fully have meant to do, ever since I have owned a copy of the book.

This old Bible was in the possession of my grandfather's second wife who had married and moved to Iowa. How the book came to be in my grandfather's hands, I do not know, but I have copied what was in it and perhaps it will help in connecting this line of the family with John I.

I remember hearing your grandfather, James Cessna, spoken of at family gatherings. Your father would be of my generation. I have four children. If there is anything further that I may be able to help concerning this branch of the family history I shall be glad to do so.

Sincerely, Gwen Cessna Price.

P. S. To letter of June 18, 1931—Gwen Price to Wanda Cessna.

William Cessna born 1777 died June 18, 1857 aged 80 years. Lies buried in Salem cemetery, Cessna Township, Hardin Co., Ohio. Keziah Cessna, his wife, whose grave is also in the same cemetery died Oct. 19, 1862 aged 69 years. Their children were: John D., James, William, George, Joseph, Zacheus, Mary Ann. John D. was the oldest child, and his descendants are given in order of their birth in the book, House of Cessna.

Clarence Cessna son of Zacheus has a will dated 1832 which was the last will and testament of James Cessna who was the father of the above William who died in 1857 aged 80 years. This James Cessna's children were: John, James, William, May, Margaret, Sarah, Elizabeth.

Howard Cessna has thought that James Cessna was the line of our branch of the family but it seems that Howard could find no trace of this James at the time he printed the book House of Cessna. Since I have seen the will dated, 1832, of James Cessna I am quite sure that he is the ancestor from which we have descended. I am quite sure if you would write to Clarence Cessna, Attorney, that he will give you a copy of the will.

In the Bible: "John Cepna was born in the year sixteen hundred and ninety-two, and died about the year seventeen hundred ninety-eight. This John was born in Ireland and the first that came to America. His father was a Frenchman. John Cepsna Bible bought seventeen hundred and ninety-one."

Mrs. Price writes that the above is written on fly leaf of the old bible which she located and is written in ink in a very legible but old-style writing. "The word Ireland was hardly discernible, but with the aid of magnifying glass I was able to read it. In the same bible, in the center of the book, at the end of the old testament, I found written in the same old style handwriting these words: 'Jonathan Cepsna was born April the first day 1789.' Then just below this I found written in a different hand-writing, very legible but much different looking style of hand-writing these words: 'Jonathan Cepsna book bought in 1820.' This book was my great-great grandfather's of Shippensburg, Pennsylvania, who lived to the age of one hundred and seven years."

I have written Clarence C. to get a copy of the will, if possible. If by any chance you have already seen a copy of it, will you let me know, as it will be unnecessary for me to send it to you, in case I am able to get it.   Sincerely,

Maude C.

August 8, 1928

Mr. Howard Cessna,
    Lutzville, Pa.

Dear Mr. Cessna: Mr. Carson, of the Mayer Aircraft was here a short time ago, bringing me the book of Cessnas, which I appreciated very highly, and wish to thank you very much for it.

I was very much interested in what Mr. Carson had to say in regard to you, and his visit on the old homestead, and would certainly have liked to have seen you myself, and if the opportunity ever presents itself, I will certainly drop in some day and make you a little visit, and extend you the cordial hand of welcome, if at any time you are close enough to Wichita to see me.

Again thanking you for the book, and your interest, in sending it down, I am   Yours very truly,

The Cessna Aircraft Company,
By C. V. Cessna, President.

237 S. Terrace Drive, Sept. 9, 1931.

Mr. Howard Cessna,
    Bedford, Pa.

Dear Cousin: It has been quite a long time since I received your last letter. I and my son, Eldon, which is the only son I have, returned from the National Air Races at Cleveland yesterday; flying from Cleveland to Wichita in eight hours and twenty minutes.

Eldon is 24 years old and for the first time entered the National Races. He won third place in the handicap race from Santa Monica, Calif. to Cleveland and also several other events at Cleveland. One of the major ones was the speed and effi-

ciency race, open to all competition, which awarded him a very
nice prize in money and a General Electric Grandfather's clock
with a radio, which is one of the latest pieces in the General Electric line.   In all he won something over $2200, in cash which is
not too bad for his first attempt; do you think?   Our business
is rather slow here in Wichita so we have been attending various
air meets, throughout the country where the prize money would
justify our attending.   However this does not make one rich as
there is a great deal of expense attached to keep up the equip-
ment and travel when racing planes.

 We all appreciated your letter and sympathy after father's
death.

 I am sure you would change your mind about flying being
dangerous if you had flown as long as I. I do not consider flying
as hazardous as traveling in automobiles on the conjested high-
ways of these times.   Flying is safe if properly conducted and
all foolishness is laid aside.   I hope sometime I will be able to
take you with me in one of our fine planes, for a little ride out
through the country.

 Mother and the rest of our immediate family are well and are
all enjoying ourselves as well as usual.   I hope this finds you and
your household likewise.

Very sincerely yours,

Clyde V. Cessna.

 P. S. I received your news article of the dedication and appreciate reading of the event; it was typical of the Cessna's, this
public life, and they usually are leaders as you perhaps have
observed.

———

JAMES CESSNA IV, JOHN III, JOHN II, JOHN I—Lived in
Cumberland County, Pennsylvania.   Left a will dated 1832,
naming as heirs (1) John, (2) Elizabeth, who married a James
Cessna, (3) May, who married John Clark, (4) Margaret, (5)
James, (6) Sarah, who married a man by name of Coffe, and
(7) William.

The House of Cessna

WILLIAM CESSNA V, JAMES IV—Born 1777 in Cumberland County, Pennsylvania. Died June 18, 1857. Lies buried in Salem Cemetery, Cessna Township, Hardin County, Ohio.

In 1828 he moved his family to Holmes County, Ohio, and in 1835 moved to what was then a wilderness, but is now Cessna Township, Hardin County, Ohio. The first schoolhouse of Cessna Township was built on his land in 1836.

He married Kesiah Davis Kyle (a widow) of Welsh ancestry. Native of Pennsylvania. She died October 19, 1862, and lies buried beside her husband William Cessna. Issue: (1) John D., (2) James, who went to Missouri, (3) Joseph, who went to California, (4) William, who went to Illinois, (5) Kesiah, who died in childhood, (6) George, Hardin County, Ohio, (7) Zaccheus, Hardin County, Ohio, (8) Mary Ann, who married Holmes Wilson, Hardin County, Ohio.

JOHN D. CESSNA IV, WILLIAM V, JAMES IV—Born February 2, 1823, in Cumberland County, Pennsylvania, moved with his parents to Holmes County, Ohio, in 1828. Moved to Cessna Township, Hardin County, Ohio, in 1835. Married Eliza Ann Reid, of English descent in 1851. During the Civil War was a volunteer in Company "G," 135th Ohio National Guard. Died January 20, 1903. Lies buried in Salem cemetery, Cessna Township, Hardin County, Ohio.

Mrs. Cessna died in 1879. Lies buried in Salem cemetery, Cessna Township, Hardin Co., Ohio. Their children were: (1) William Manley, (2) Mary Elizabeth, who married William Miller, farmer and road contractor of Hardin County, Ohio. She died in 1932. Issue: Anna Rose and Harriet. (3) Zaccheus Phillips, single, died in Merriam, Kansas, 1931; (4) Albert Clement, who went to Washington State, married, and died there; (5) George Henry, who married Anna Stewart, and lives in Merriam, Kansas. Mrs. Cessna died in 1928. Issue: Della Byrd, who married William West and lives in Merriam, Kansas. (6) John David, married in Rosedale, Kansas, died there in 1933. Had one son, Phillip. (7) Harriet Ann married James M. Hively, a farmer in Cessna Township, Hardin County, Ohio.

Issue: (1) John D., single, (2) Carrie A., (3) Wilbur J., who died in childhood.

Second marriage was in 1881 to Lyda Ann Obenour, native of Ohio. Issue: (1) Bessie Carrie, who married Elmer Davis and lives on a farm in Hardin County, Ohio; (2) Meredith Merril, who received military training at Fort Riley, Kansas, being Sergeant in Troop C, 1st Cavalry. During the World War, he was Captain of 2nd Cavalry Training Troop, at Chissay, France. He is married and lives in Texas; (3) Clyde Chester, California.

WILLIAM MANLEY CESSNA VII, JOHN D. VI, WILLIAM V—Born November 7, 1852. Died October 19, 1918, married Clara Belle Davis, born June 15, 1855. She died October 9, 1894. They lie buried in Salem cemetery, Cessna Township, Hardin County, Ohio. Issue: (1) Carl, who died in infancy; (2) Ray Henry, (3) Anna Gail, (4) Gwendoline, (5) Mary Cathleen, (6) Harriet Belle.

Second marriage in 1896 to Emma Long. Issue: (1) Lorna, (2) John, (3) Doris.

RAY HENRY CESSNA VIII, WILLIAM MANLEY VII—Born December 23, 1877. Died November 3, 1920. He was a Sergeant in Company I, 41st Infantry, U. S. A. in the Spanish-American War and served two years in the Phillipine Islands. His health became impaired during his service from which he never recovered.

ANNA GAIL CESSNA VIII, WILLIAM MANLEY VII—Born June 16, 1880. Address Westerville, Ohio. Married Franklin B. Howe in 1903. Issue: (1) Norman Frederick, (2) Zilpah Pauline, (3) Martha Ann, (4) Isabel. Norman Howe, sales manager in Los Angeles, Calif. Married. Zilpah Pauline Howe, school teacher, Westerville, Ohio. Martha Ann Howe, student at Otterbein College, Westerville, Ohio. Isabel Howe, student in high school, Westerville, Ohio.

GWENDOLINE CESSNA VIII, WILLIAM MANLEY VII—Born February 22, 1884. Address Forest, Ohio. Married William Bradley Price, attorney-at-law. Issue: (1) Russell Cessna, (2) Bradley, (3) Eloise, (4) Harry Manley.

The House of Cessna

RUSSELL CESSNA PRICE IX, GWENDOLINE CESSNA VIII—Born July 8, 1904. Address Upper Sandusky, Ohio. At present with Federal Land Bank, Louisville, Ky. Occupation, attorney at law. Married Hilda E. Kimmel. Issue: (1) Russell Eugene, (2) William Bradley.

BRADLEY PRICE IX, GWENDOLINE CESSNA VIII—Born Mar. 30, 1906. Address Lansing, Michigan. Single. Occupation, Sales Manager.

ELOISE PRICE IX, GWENDOLINE VIII—Born November 16, 1908. Address Forest, Ohio. Occupation, teacher of French and music in Forest, Ohio, High School.

HARRY MANLEY PRICE IX, GWENDOLINE VIII—Born Oct. 26, 1914. Address Forest, Ohio. Student of Miami University, Oxford, Ohio.

MARY CATHLEEN CESSNA VIII, WILLIAM MANLEY VII—Born February 21, 1887. Address Columbus, Ohio. Occupation, School nurse.

HARRIET BELLE CESSNA VIII, WILLIAM MANLEY VII—Born March 5, 1889. Address Westerville, Ohio. Married George Shaw Meyer. Issue: (1) George Shaw, Jr., student Otterbein College, Westerville, Ohio; (2) Mary Margaret, student in High School, Westerville, Ohio.

LORNA CESSNA KIDD VIII, WILLIAM MANLEY VII—Born January 26, 1904. Married Clyde Kidd. Address Forest, Ohio. Issue: (1) Clyde, Jr., (2) Thomas, (3) Nelson.

JOHN CESSNA VIII, WILLIAM MANLEY VII—Born February 7, 1905. Address Columbus, Ohio. Single.

DORIS CESSNA VIII, WILLIAM MANLEY VII—Born February 4, 1909. Address Columbus, Ohio. Occupation, stenographer.

HE'S A "FLY" FARMER—CHARLIE CESSNA, OUT IN KANSAS, MARKETS EGGS IN AEROPLANE—SCORNS A HORSE AND BUGGY— ONE SUNDAY, JUST AS PARSON WAS PRAYING FOR VISITATION OF ANGEL HOST, CESSNA SWOOPED DOWN AND BROKE UP MEETING.

Now and then readers of the weekly paper out in Hutchinson, Kansas, discover some such item as this:

"C. V. Cessna made a flying trip to Kingman yesterday," or, "Charlie Cessna dropped in at Norwich to attend the lyceum Thursday evening."

All of which statements are literally correct, for Cessna is one Kingman county farmer boy who has gone his neighbors one better in solving the problem of rural transportation. When other farmers in the township discarded their old carriage teams for touring cars, Cessna took to a flying machine. Now he does his marketing in a French monoplane.

Cessna lives near Belmont, on the Missouri Pacific railroad, but there is only one slow train a day each way, and roads are an uncertain proposition much of the time. Therefore it seemed that there was only one way for a progressive farmer like Charlie ever to get anywhere, and that was by the air line.

One Sunday morning, shortly after he had received his monoplane, Cessna spruced up and flew to church at the Adams circuit meeting house. Elder Jenkins was in the midst of a powerful prayer. He was just calling upon the angelic host to unfold their wings and hover about, when a mighty whirring was heard and a huge birdlike apparition was seen swooping down from the sky, headed straight for the church. Cessna did not attend the services; for when he arrived, the meeting had broken up.

Cessna has a vein of humor. One of his little jokes is to fly to some near-by town to attend the county fair or a baseball game, and just fly over the fence without consulting the gate keeper. Of course he's always welcome, and he's the only man who has the complete and unabridged privilege of climbing the fence whenever he feels like it.

FOUR SONS OF LATE J. W. CESSNA HANDLED DETAILS OF FUNERAL—PREPARED BODY, TOOK CHARGE OF SERVICES AND ACTED AS PALLBEARERS—WISHES OF THE FATHER.

From the time he became dangerously ill until his body was laid in a grave near his home, J. W. Cessna, a pioneer resident of Kansas, had the personal care of four of his five sons. The funeral of Mr. Cessna was unusual since the sons prepared the body for burial, took active charge of the service, acted as pallbearers and filled the grave.

Although Mr. Cessna died several days ago and was buried near the place he homesteaded in Kingman county, it was only learned yesterday his every wish concerning his funeral had been carried out by the sons. The sons are Clyde V. Cessna, Wichita aircraft builder; Roy Cessna, Ulysses; Bert Cessna, prominent banker at Ingels; and Noel Cessna, who lives on the family place nine miles west of Norwich. Another son, Pearl Cessna, who resides in Saskatchewan, Canada, was unable to be present.

Mr. Cessna was 74 years old. He had not been in good health for some time, but up until five or six days before he died he had been active about his home. He settled on the Kingman county farm in 1880 and became a much respected citizen in that community. According to his son, Clyde, Mr. Cessna many times told members of his family how he wished to be buried. It was his desire that his sons take charge of all the details. This was done to the letter.

Mr. Cessna is survived by his wife and two daughters in addition to the five sons. The daughters, Mrs. Grace Wallace, Norwich, and Mrs. Hazel Herman, Pittsburgh, Pa., were present for the funeral.

The Cessna children were at the bedside when their father breathed his last. At once the sons took charge. They embalmed the body and placed it in the coffin. When the funeral service was held at the Methodist church in Norwich the brothers carried the casket into the church. After the service, which was conducted in the usual manner by a minister, Bert Cessna spoke a few words as relatives and friends stood with bowed heads.

With steady hands and firm steps the four sons lifted the casket and placed it in a hearse. At the cemetery one of the sons gave a short prayer as the body was lowered into the grave. When the casket was resting in the ground the sons stood silently by for a few minutes. Then with shovels they covered the grave.

Many friends of the family looked on at the funeral service

and burial. And many were moved to remark they never could have pictured a more splendid tribute to a father than that tendered by the sons of this Kansas pioneer.

Last night Clyde Cessna, in recalling the words of his father, said: "It was just as he wished. We talked it over and decided we could perform all the tasks, even to preparing the body. We did not intend to attract attention by so doing, but were doing as we thought father wanted us to do. He always had expressed a desire to be buried in a modest manner."

WILLS, JOHN CESSNA, AND JAMES SISNA, INVENTORY STEPHEN SISNA

Orphans Court records of Sisney children minors. Deeds Stephen Cisney, a second of the name. Cumberland County, Pennsylvania.

Will of *John Cessna*, Will Book "F" page 40, Cumberland County, Pennsylvania Office of Register of Wills, Carlisle.

In the name of God Amen! I John Cessna of Shippensburg in the county of Cumberland, and state of Pennsylvania being weak in body, but of sound and perfect mind and memory through God's blessing, and calling to mind, that it is appointed for all men once to die, do make and publish this my last will and testament, in manner and form following that is to say— First I give my soul to God who gave it me, and my body to the dust to be buried in a decent manner at the discretion of my Executors, and I order that all my just debts and personal charges be paid as soon as may be out of my estate.

Imprimis, I give and bequeath unto my eldest son John Cessna, my sons Charles Cessna, Joseph Cessna, Jonathan Cessna, deceased, Evan Cessna, William Cessna, and my eldest daughter Mary Neale, deceased, my other daughters Elizabeth Jones and Margaret Hall, deceased, the sum of five shillings each which said sum of five shillings is to be paid, within one year after my decease, each of the above named my sons and daughters, unto each of their heirs if demanded legally, that is the heirs of either of the above named my sons and daughters who are or may be dead before said legacy of five shillings be paid to them, shall jointly receive the said sum, divided amongst them, which said sum of five shillings, together with what they have already received in land or cash, to be in full for their several shares, out of my estate, any particular law or usage to the contrary notwithstanding, they having heretofore received their and each of their full share, from me or what I allowed to be as such and to my youngest son Theophelus Cessna, I give the sum of five shillings, to be paid in one year after my decease, which with what I have already given to be in full for his share out of my estate or estates.

Item—I give and bequeath unto my son James Cessna, all my house and lots in Shippensburg, with all my rights and titles to each of them, also a tract of land in Southampton township, bounded as described in a conveyance from William Campbell with all the appurtenances belonging to the said tract of land. Also a tract of land warranted and surveyed lying on Juniata Creek or river, above Jack's Narrows now supposed to be in Huntingdon County, also my right in and to a five shilling warrant taken out of the late Proprietaries Office for an island in Juniata river, and another having an older right for it, the said warrant was renewed and laid on the land adjoining the river, and including the land where Prigmore's mill is now built. Also all my right of a grant of land I got from Mr. Blunston's lying near Susquehanna river, on the west side in York County, near Conewago creek, an adjoining the same as may appear by said grant to have and to hold the above mentioned lots tracts of land, warrants with all my interest of, in, or therein, and each of them mentioned or intended to be mentioned to the said James Cessna, his heirs and assigns forever, subject nevertheless to the payment of the several legacies herein mentioned before and after this clause. Also I give and bequeath unto the said James Cessna, all my right and title, in and to a certain quantity of back land taken up and surveyed in partnership with Messeurs Hutton (?) and Wallace, with all my accounts against said partnerships to be held by my said son James, my full moiety or share that may fall to me on a division, and by his heirs and assigns forever as fully as I could have held the same.

Item—I give and bequeath unto my grand daughter Elizabeth Cessna, daughter to William Cessna, all my right, of, in, or to, that piece of land warranted and surveyed adjoining the place formerly Robert Gabney's on the south and lands of Samuel Culbertson it being a piece of land that I bought of Nathaniel Wilson deceased, but I order and it is my will that my son James Cessna, if he thinks it best shall have full power and authority to sell and convey said tract of land to the best advantage and place the money out at interest for said Elizabeth Cessna until she shall arrive at the age of twenty one (21) years but if it should not be sold before she arrives at the age of twenty one years (21) then it shall be held by Elizabeth Cessna her heirs and assigns forever. And I do further order and direct, that after my said son James Cessna, has paid the before mentioned legacies that, then the remainder and reversions of all and singular, my estates, real and personal, shall be and I do hereby bequeath and devise all lands, back accounts, warrants for land, or lands, not beforementioned in whatever place situate, that may appear to be my right unto my said son James Cessna, as fully as if they had been mentioned to him his heirs and assigns forever. Hereby constituting and appointing him my sole Executor to this my last will and testament and also give my said Executors, all my whole power toward Executing or assuring any other conveyance or conveyances, that may be wanting to confirm my tract of land heretofore granted or conveyed by me as also my whole power to act or to sign, seal, covey or make complete anything that I am bound to do by any article or covenant and not already done as full as I could have done in my life time.

Hereunto revoking and disannulling all other wills and testaments by me made ordaining this or other to be my last will and testament as witness my hand and seal this twenty fourth day of October in the year of our Lord, seventeen ninety-three (1793).

Note: Be it be remembered that if the above mentioned Elizabeth Cessna should die without issue before she arrives at the age of twenty one years that the above legacy shall go to her brother John Cessna.

Signed, sealed, published and pronounced by the testator as his last will and testament in presence of us who also signed the same as witness at the request of, and in the presence of the testator and of each other, Matthew Scott, John Henry, John Scott.   —John Cessna

Will of *James Cessna*, Book "K" Page 354, Cumberland County, Pennsylvania, Office of Register of Wills at Carlisle.

In the name of God Amen!

I James Cessna, of Southampton township, Cumberland County, am frail of body though of sound mind, memory and understanding, blessed be God for the same do make and ordain the following to be my last will and testament in manner and form, that is to say I give my soul to God who gave it and I order and direct that my body be interred in the earth in a decent like manner. Item—I order and direct that my beloved wife Mary be supported out of my estate in a descent like manner during her natural life. Item—I order and direct that my estate both real and personal, be sold by my Executors herein after named, as soon as conveniently may be after my decease, and all my lawful debts and funeral expenses be paid. Item—I give and bequeath to my son John Cessna, one dollar in full for his share out of my estate both real and personal. Item—I will and bequeath to my son James Cessna, five hundred dollars over and above what is hereinafter bequeathed to him out of my estate.

Item—I give and bequeath to my daughter Elizabeth Cisna, intermarried with James Cisna fifty dollars to be in full for her share. I give and bequeath to John Clark who was intermarried to my daughter Mary, one dollar, to be in full for his share. Item—It is my will and I do order and direct, that the residue and remainder of my estate not herein before bequeathed be divided in four equal shares (that is) I will and bequeath to my son William Cisna one share, I give and bequeath to my daugh-

ter Margaret Cisna, one share, I give and bequeath to my son
James Cisna, one share, over and above what is hereinbefore bequeathed to him, I give and bequeath to my grand children, that
is the children of my daughter Sarah who was intermarried with
Thomas Coffee—viz Mary Coffee—intermarried with Peter
Fogle, Robert Coffee, James Coffee, and John Coffee, one share
to be equally divided between them.   Item—I nominate and appoint my son James Cisna, to be Guardian over the estates of
my grand children and hereby authorize him to purchase land
for them with their share.   And lastly I nominate and appoint
my son James Cissna to be whole and sole Executor of this my
last will and testament and I hereby authorize him to make a
good title, for my real estate as good as I could do was I living
when the same is sold.   In witness whereof I have hereunto set
my hand and seal, the 8th day of May A. D. one thousand eight
hundred and thirty-two.   Signed James Sisna.

Witnesses: Benjamin Duke, Jacob Stineman, Jacob Kiser.

CUMBERLAND COUNTY CESSNA—SISNEY RECORDS

No trace whatever appears under either the Cessna, Cisna or
Sisney spelling of a will, administration or any deed of a Thomas
Cessna in Cumberland County.

Under the heading of *Stephen Sisna*, with no residence location, nor any date of letters there follows only the date of the
Inventory of the estate viz April 18th, 1763 and no final ac-
county was filed.

However reference to the Inventor is interesting and allumi-
nating as to the date of death of Stephen Sisna.   The form of
the Inventor is as follows, viz:

"Inventor appraisement of the goods and chattels belonging
to Stephen Sisna, deceased, August 31st, 1756

1 cow............................2 ℔	15 sh	
1 *Chist*.................................	5 sh	
1 small box.....................	2 sh	6 d
To putter ....1 ℔	5 sh	
1 small tea kettle.........		

The House of Cessna

```
To one old bed............        3 sh
A small pot...............        2 sh        6 d
                                 ____  ____
     Total..............7 ℔       9 sh
```

Inventor file "S" number 19.

Appraised by us, James Boggs, William Piper, April 18th, 1763.

Deeds show that one Stephen Cisney, bought of John Gardner two lots or tracts of land in Toboyne township, one Nov. 16th, 1796 and one Sept. 2nd, 1796 one 50 acres and one 48 acres. He paid fifty pounds for the 50 acres and 150 pounds for the 48 acres and 14 perches. Stephen Cisney then lived when purchase was made in Toboyne township. Book M Vol. 1, pages 34 and 3.

We find in 1793 one John Cessna buying land in Shippensburg for $200 lot number 18. John Cessna in this deed is designated as "John Cessna, the elder" Book K Vol. 1, page 562.

A Sheriff's deed Stephen Sessna to William Russell dated April 18th, 1758 Vol. 1, Book O, page 459 (evidently of estate of Stephen) explains why there was no estate for division.

Orphans Court record Book 1, page 88, and the same record found in Book 2, page 28 says:

At an Orphans Court held in Carlisle for the County of Cumberland, 25th of August, 1763 came into Court Patience Sisny and praysed that Guardians be appointed over the person and estates of Stephen, and John Sisney, minor orphans sons of John Sisney deceased and Stephen Sisney son to Thomas Sisney during their minority. Court upon due consideration appointed William Smith, Esq., Guardian of the three children during their minorities.

CHAPTER XI

Stephen Cessna, Brother of Maj. John Cessna—His Descendants

Portland, Oregon, July 5th, 1931.

Mr. Howard Cessna,
 Lutzville, Pa.

Dear Mr. Cessna: I am taking the liberty to trouble you again.

As you will probably recall, I wrote you a couple of months ago and am trying to trace my family history in order to become a member of the D. A. R.

I wrote Mrs. Blosser at Chillicothe, Ohio, as you advised. I sent her a check for $5.00, at her request, and am to pay her another $5.00 if she succeeds in getting any results. She uses this money for D. A. R. purposes.

I knew that my great grandfather, John Cissna, had died there about 1820. She established the fact that he died there Sept. 3rd, 1821, at the age of 42 years. I have since verified this fact from two old family bibles that I did not know were in existence and which are in the possession of relatives of my father.

I thought perhaps great grandfather, John Cissna, was a son of Stephen III of Chillicothe. I think now it is more likely that he was a nephew. From cousins of my father, who are much older than I, I have learned that my great grandfather was married in Pittsburgh, Pa., about 1799, and his eldest son, Robert Cissna, was born there in 1800. As my grandfather, Charles Cissna, was born in Chillicothe in 1808, my great grandfather moved there between 1800 and 1808. As he was 42 when he died there in 1821, that makes him born in 1779.

What I am trying to establish is where he was born and who his father was.

Upon the advice of the State Regent of the D. A. R. for

Oregon, I wrote the State Regent at Philadelphia, also the State Libraries at Harrisburg, Pa. Two months ago I wrote the County Clerk at Pittsburgh, and although I enclosed a stamped envelope, I have never received any reply.

Could you suggest anything further that I could do?

I wrote also to Miss Sarah Frances Cissna at Watseka, Ill. I learned that she had passed away July 29th, 1924.

I have received a letter from her niece, Mrs. Georgia C. Bester, 6024 Swope Parkway, Kansas City, Mo., she could give me no additional information. She said her aunt's book "House of Cessna" came into her possession at her aunt's death.

If there are any suggestions you could make, I would appreciate it greatly.

Thanking you in advance and enclosing a stamped envelope, I remain,

Very sincerely yours,

Grace Cissna Guthrie

Portland, Oregon, May 26, 1931.

Dear Mr. Cessna: Thank you so much for the information you sent me and also for the Pamphlet.

I sent the pamphlet to Charles J. Cissna, at Fort Scott, Kansas. He is a double cousin of my father's He has a son, Volney Cissna, in New York City, who is an electrical engineer, in the employ of the Electric Bond & Share Co.

He is planning on visiting his son this summer in New York, and if he does so, may possibly go through Bedford and may call on you.

I am writing Mrs. Blosser at Chillicothe, Ohio, as you suggested and will try to get in touch with Sarah Frances Cissna, or some of her relatives, at Watseka, Ill.

Since writing you, I have learned that my great grandfather Cissna died about 1820 in Chillicothe, Ohio, but as yet I do not know his first name. He was married in Pittsburgh, Pa., sometime between 1800 and 1807, but I do not know my great grandmother's maiden name.

I am trying to get definite information on this point now. I have written the County Clerk at Pittsburgh, but to date have had no reply.

Thank you for your kind invitation to call on you, but I am not planning any trip east at present.

If you have never been in Oregon, you are missing a great deal. No doubt you have heard of Portland as being the "Rose City," and you have perhaps heard of our famous "Columbia Highway."

My husband and myself extend you a cordial invitation to visit Portland and to accept our hospitality if you do so.

Sincerely yours,
Grace Cissna Guthrie

Reeder Hotel, Tulsa, Okla.

Mr. Howard Cessna,
  Bedford, Pa.

Dear Cousin: Yours of recent date enclosing letter from Dr. H. E. Harman, was received in due time and I am hereby returning same to you, after taking a copy.

My grandfather, James had three brothers, Charles, William, and Robert, all older than he. Samuel of Washington Court House, O., was a son of Robert. He had a brother John who at one time had a hotel in Washington Court House, O. William had a son John L. who lived in Nodaway County, Mo. The descendants of Charles live in Portland, Ore. According to my information, Robert was at one time Sheriff of Fayette Co., Ohio.

Yours,
Charles G. Cissna.

Fairfield, Ill., Dec. 13, 1929.

Mr. Howard Cessna,
  Everett, Pa.

Dear Sir: I married into the Cessna family 36 years ago. My

Grandfather evans Cissna Road
brother James (b. 1796)

The House of Cessna

wife's name was Mame C. Cissna. Her father's name was John Wesley Cissna and grandfather's name was James Cissna. Great grandfather's name was either John or Jonathan. Wife says her father always said there was a John or Jonathan in every generation. My wife's father came from Ohio to Wayne County, Illinois when a young man with his father and mother. My father died several years ago and she don't seem to remember very much about her father's people. My wife's father had one brother whose name was James Cissna, and some of the Cissnas lived in Pennsylvania. Some of the Cissnas spelled their name Cefsna and Cessna. She said she had seen some of her father's writing and he spelled his name sometimes with an "f," Cefsna. I have been told by someone that you have books for sale giving the genealogy of the Cessna family. I would like very much to have one of these for my children, if they do not cost too much. I have them on my side of the family, and the children would like one from their mother's side.

Yours very truly,

O. C. Fogle.

Fairfield, Ill., May 17, 1931.

Mr. Howard Cessna,
Bedford, Pa.

Dear Sir: I received the book of the ceremonies of the dedication of Major John A. Cessna. Many thanks. My wife will write you in a few days. I am enclosing an old record that was contracted between my wife's father and his brother in 1844. It is not clear to my wife just where she comes in the Cissna family. I heard my wife's mother say one time the ground where Cissna Park is located belongs to my wife's father's brother.

I am enclosing a small Genealogy of the Fogle family for you to give to the Mr. Fogle you mentioned in one of your letters to me. Thought perhaps if we were related he might help me out some, as my people first settled in Pennsylvania and Maryland.

If you are ever out this way would be glad to have you stop and make us a visit.

Yours very truly,

O. C. Fogle.

Box 94, Chillicothe, Ohio.

Thought you would be interested in the enclosed.

When I went to place a bouquet of old fashioned white roses on Stephen's grave yesterday, the sexton said "hundreds have come to that grave today." I had a list of Revolutionary soldiers and place of burial in one paper and a list of 147 War of 1812 soldiers in this country in another—all located by me, and most of them marked. I have several others ready to add, so you see I am not wasting much time.

Kathryn D. Blosser.

Fairfield, Ill., May 23, 1931.

Mr. Howard Cessna,
Bedford, Pa.

Dear Mr. Cessna: I am very much interested in tracing my line of the Cessna ancestry but I fear you will think differently since I let my husband do the writing to gather information. I know so little of my father's family to help clear the line of descent. His father's name was James—his mother's name was Katherin Ewing—he had one brother James, sisters named Margaret, Mary Jane, Rebecca and Elizabeth. All married and lived in Illinois, except Mary Jane Grant, who lived and died in Colorado. My grandfather's family came to Wayne County, Ill., from Ohio, but I don't know just where, but presume since seeing your "House of Cessna," from Chillicothe. My father at one time visited in Ohio after his mother had been taken to Cincinnati for an operation but it was before my time, so don't know where they visited. I have heard my father say the Cissna who founded "Cessna Park" was his relative—an uncle, if I remember right. But I didn't see how that could be, for the House of Cessna records Stephen and William as the only descendants of Steven (of the War of 1812). The Steven Cissna's picture on page 104 looks as much like my father as if it were his picture. My daughters are very much interested in tracing our line and to learn if they are eligible for the D. A. R's.

I thank you for all the information you have given me and the books of the dedication services of the Major John Cessna Tablet. I don't want to be greedy, but each of my daughters would like one of these small books—with the one you so kindly sent today, two more will be enough.

My brother John mentioned in your House of Cessna, is now living in San Antonio, Texas, 238 Porter Street. Think I forgot to mention my father's name—John Wesley Cissna.

Sister to
Bess Cissna Handley

Sincerely,

Mame Cissna Fogle.

The Cissna on page 104—about same age of my wife's father, about 4 years difference in ages.

Portland, Ore., Jan. 31, 1929.
281 East 14th Street North

Mr. Howard Cessna,
Rainsburg, Penna.

Dear Sir: I have been informed that you have published a book concerning the Cessna family. If such is the case, will you kindly inform me where I may obtain a copy, the price, etc.

My father's name was John Robert Cissna, which I understand is a corruption of the original name DeCessna.

He was born at Pt. Pleasant, Ohio, in 1842. I understand our branch is not included in the Volume, but would like the book anyway.

Yours very truly,

Mrs. Mary Cissna Wilson.

Ontario, Ore., Sept. 24, 1934.

Mr. Howard Cessna,
Bedford, Pa.

Dear Sir: My brother, Charley G. Cissna, wrote me a short time ago about receiving a card from you stating that you were planning on putting out a new edition of the family book, providing you get sufficient response to warrant it. I would like to have one.

I believe I am to send you two dollars for same, which you will find enclosed.

Sincerely,

Edith Cissna Cooper.

Box 94, Chillicothe, O., Dec. 27, 1929.

Mr. Howard Cessna,
Bedford, Pa.

My dear Mr. Cessna: Although it is a long time since I was in Bedford, I have not forgotten my then conceived idea of looking for Cessna records in Ross County, and sending them to you. So, I have stolen moments now and then, and am sending you a few results.

The kodak picture shows the graves of Stephen and John. On Stephen's stone is the following: "In Memory of Stephen Cissna who was born July the 20th, 1737 and died August the 14th, 1823."

On John's stone: "In Memory of John Cisna who died Sept. 3rd, 1821, aged 42 years

> With heavenly Weapons he hath
> Fought, the Battles of the Lord
> Finished his cors and kept the
> Faith, and gained the great Reward."

I looked in the probate court but neither left a will. Margaret Cissna was appointed administratrix of Stephen's estate Sept. 23, 1823 and gave bond for $300, but those are the only

The House of Cessna

papers on file in connection with the estate. I have not had time to go to recorder's office. We are building an addition to our court house and among the new apartments will be more extensive vaults for probate records, joined to the present rooms, so it is not particularly easy to do much in there right now.

I regretted so much not to see your Cessna book. We were in Bedford a week, but time always flies, and a week is very short to do all one would like.

Forgot to call your attention to the bronze marker at Stephen's grave. I placed that, and on Memorial Day there is always a flag—and flowers there, too.

With best wishes to you and Mrs. Cessna, I am,

Sincerely,

(Mrs. Peter J.) Kathryn D. Blosser.

Stephen was with 1st Regiment that marched from here and took part in the Battle of Bunker Hill. See my Book, page 100.

Some where is a letter in which he said after the War he had gone through h - - -. He was a sharp shooter, able to hit the bulls eye 250 yards.

Chillicothe, Ohio, April 29, 1933.

Mr. Howard Cessna,
Bedford, Pa.

Dear Sir: Thank you for your letter of April 27th and for the Harman information you sent. Any other data you may find will be appreciated. Do your records tell anything about the founders of Harmanville, Bedford County, Pa.?

In the Probate Court records (Ross County) I found where Margaret Cissna was appointed administrator of the estate of Stephen Cissna Sept. 23, 1823. On the same date Margaret Cissna, Samuel Long and Samuel Porter signed as surities on a $300.00 bond. There was no further record of the administration of the estate. That was the only record in that office. In the Recorders office I found where Stephen Cissna and wife bought and sold several pieces of property in Chillicothe and

Clarksburg (Ross County) between 1810 and 1823. These pieces were not bought from or sold to anyone by the name of Cissna. Also in the Recorders Office I found the following Cissnas: John, Samuel, Joseph P., Adrian, Charles, Robert and William. A record of a deed signed by Stephen and William Cissna of Warren County, Indiana, in 1846 was also found. I could find nothing to show the names of Stephen Cissna or any record of transfer of property through a will. The Stephen Cissna you mentioned is buried in Chillicothe and his grave was marked by the local D. A. R. Chapter about two years ago. I can get the information from his stone if you desire it.

If there is anything else I can look up for you, let me know.

Sincerely,

Howard E. Harman.

238 Porter, San Antonio, Texas,

Mr. Howard Cessna,

R. D. 4, Bedford, Penna.

Dear Cousin: My sister, Mrs. O. C. Fogle, Fairfield, Illinois, informs me you are having another Cessna book published. Since I have had no notice of such a book in the making, I am assuming that there will be little data concerning our particular branch of the family included; and ask that you send one of the books to me at the above address, where I have living for the past fifteen years. Have been connected with the Quartermaster's Department at Fort Sam Houston for the past 17 years.

Another sister, Mrs. J. B. Handley, formerly of Fairfield and Champaign, Illinois, is also living here now, since the decease of my wife, two years ago. We are the three children of John Wesley and Emily Cissna. Ira James Cissna, son of James Cissna (brother of our father, John Wesley) is alo living in San Antonio. One of his sisters, Mrs. Julia Ritter is living in Fairfield, Illinois and the other sister, Mrs. Cora Howerth (wife of Professor I. W. Howerth) lives in Greenley, Colorado.

Sincerely yours,

July 18, 1934. John A. Cissna

The House of Cessna

Ottawa, Ill., May 9th, 1933.

Mr. Howard Cessna,
    Bedford, Pennsylvania.

Dear Sir: I have a copy of a letter which C. G. Cissna of Kansas City, Kansas, wrote to my daughter, Mrs. Virgil Riek, of Jefferson City, Missouri, in which he states that you have compiled a Genealogy of the Cissna Family and issued a book on the same.

Do you have any copies of this book left which you can spare? If so, please advise me as to the price you ask for the same. If you do not have any copies to spare, would it be possible to borrow a copy of your book, if I will be careful of it and return it to you in good condition promptly. I would like to have permission to copy such portions of it as I may need for purposes of my search.

My grandmother was a daughter of Jonathan Cissna who died about 60 years ago in Iowa. He lived for a great many years in Indiana and I think he moved to that state from Ohio. I think there was a Stephen Cissna who was very closely related to him. I may be wrong, but my recollection is that grandmother told me that he was either a brother or a half-brother of her father's.

Hoping that I may have the pleasure of hearing from you at your earliest convenience, I am,

           Yours very cordially,
               Homer H. Hankins,
                 Deputy Co. Recorder.

Kansas City, Kans., June 12, 1924.

Mr. Howard Cessna,
    Bedford, Pennsylvania.

My Dear Sir: While in Los Angeles in February I dropped in at the shop of a Mrs. Cessna on Seventh Street in that city, and through her became interested in a book for which you are responsible, "The House of Cessna." I have intended ever since then to write to you in regard to it. I had never met the lady before but was led to stop by the name that appeared on the window. I also visited Mr. Sam Cessna of Los Angeles where I saw the book before mentioned, and Mrs. Serowinsky of Venice, California about whom I learned through the Mrs. Cessna.

My branch of the family seems to have been lost some two or three generations back, I was unable to determine just where, so I decided to tell you what I know and see if you are able to gather up any loose threads.

My great grandfather's name was John Cissna, who lived in Ohio, I think, for a time at least, in or about Chillicothe. He died about 1821. I will name his sons as accurately as I can, they were, Charles, Robert, John, and James; there were also two daughters, one named Rose, the other I do not recall. James Cissna was my grandfather, he was born in Ohio about 1818, he was a saddle maker by trade, lived for a time in Salem, Ill., afterward moved to Hunt Co., Texas, where he lived at the time of the Civil War, later he moved to Bourbon Co., Kansas, where he lived till his death in 1892. James has two sons and one daughter all living, Robert, Charles, and Rose; Robert has four sons, of which I am one, and three daughters living. Charles has one son and one daughter.

I am inclined to think from what I could gather from this book, that our line would lead back to Stephen IV.

Sam Cissna of Washington Court House, Ohio, a retired banker is a first cousin of my father, being a son of one of the brothers of James.

My father has a small bible which was given by his grandmother to his father, James, in which the text used at the funeral of John Cissna is mentioned, also the name of the minister officiating.

If you are able to connect this with any information you already have, or if I can give any further information, I would be glad to hear from you.

Yours truly,

C. G. Cissna.

The House of Cessna

P. S.: We have a Cissna Street in Kansas City, Kansas. I do not know who is responsible for it.   C. G. C.

Jefferson City., Mo., May 2, 1933.

Mr. Howard Cessna,
  Bedford, Pennsylvania.

I do not know much more about my DeCissna line than I did at the time I last wrote you a month ago but a few meager facts have shown up that may help find my line.

I have abandoned the idea that Jonathan of Louisville of your line is my lost ancestor. The Louisville records had no record of marriage of Jonathan to Susan Beechler. Of course that means little.

I found two books in the St. Louis reference library on the early days of Louisville and it mentioned not one Cessna, Cissna, de or otherwise, and gave a picture of the first house built in Louisville and name of builder. I hope they are wrong for the sake of your findings.

I seem to have been wrong about the name of my great, great grandfather. Instead of Jonathan, it was John. His Revolutionary grandfather was Jonathan Alexander Pinkerton De Cessna. Both of these statements are purely legendary. Now my facts stand:

Jonathan Alexander Pinkerton DeCessna children known from graves.

John, Rebecca, Joseph (there were others).

Joseph had a daughter Rebecca know because of a grave in Sigourney, Iowa.

John married Susan Beechler who is buried near Girard, Ohio. Their children as far as I can determine were Ann Jane, my great grandmother (possibly on record as Ann or Jane) who married William Randall; Mary who married a doctor Selby; Susan who married James Adams; George and John. Probably there were others. Susan was buried recently in California; Mary, a few years ago in the Nett eton Home Cemetery at K. C., Mo. Ann Jane died and was buried in Sigourney, Iowa in December 1922.

It rather appears to me-that Mr. C. G. Cissna who referred me to you and I are working on the same line, that is if he happens to be Guy Cissna of our line.   An aunt wrote me yesterday that the brothers of my great grandmother Ann Jane, (George) had children, Guy of Kansas City, Mo., Ethel, and Fay.   The last named by a second wife.   When I wrote him I did not identify myself as a Hankins, and since I called the father of George and Ann Jane Jonathan instead of John there was nothing to indicate that we were both lost in the same trial.   In case you have developed anything through his facts, that may throw light on my situation.

I wish I could have the early facts from your book, concerning the family.   Would it be too much trouble?

Yours very truly,
Mrs. Virgil Riek.

How much data has Mrs. Eleanor Van Evern of San Diego and what is her address?

Jefferson City, Mo., March 21, 1933.

Mr. Howard Cessna,
   Attorney at Law
      Bedford, Pennsylvania.

Dear Sir: I have a copy of a very interesting letter of yours of 1932, to C. G. Cissna of Kansas City, sent to me in response to an inquiry I made of him last week concerning the early history of your family.

My great grandmother Randall, was before her marriage Ann Jane DeCessna, born April 1, 1832, daughter of Jonathan DeCessna and wife Susan (?) Beechler.   Jonathan DeCessna was (reputedly) Jonathan Alexander Pinkerton DeCessna, a Revolutionary officer.   Tradition has it that he was the first white child born in Detroit but after a careful investigation of library and court house records in Detroit I considered this an error, but I imagine he was the first white child born *some place* that later became a city of note.   It is also the family story that he was riding his mount in battle and the horse was shot from under him. His son Jonathan was said to have been stolen by the Indians and raised by them I have no verification of the stories told by my grandmother (great) but she was a very clear thinking old woman and very accurate in her mental processes to-the last. She died at ninety one.

I understand that you have written a book on your family and I am very anxious to trace mine. Is it asking too much of you to determine from your records if my family ties up with yours? I firmly believe that Cissna, and Cessna families have corrupted the name of DeCissna and have a common source. Even in our family there is a dispute as to whether great grandmother Randall called herself Cissna or Cessna before her marriage to William Randall. She said Cissna, but others claim Cessna.

Do you think it possible that the "John's" of your line are diminutives of "Jonathan?"

Is it at all probable that there was a DeCissna and a DeCessna family both?

If you can give me a lead on this I will certainly be obliged to you and will be glad to assist you in any matter possible.

Our Supreme Court Library abounds with information concerning early families in New Jersey, Rhode Island, Connecticut, Illinois and Massachussetts and I would be only too glad to hunt up anything you might be interested in, in return for your help.

Respectfully,

Mrs. Virgil Riek,

710 West Washington Avenue,
Council Bluffs, Iowa,
April 9th, 1934.

Mr. Howard Cessna,
Bedford, Pennsylvania.

Dear Sir: Yours of the 24th of March received, and am very much pleased to hear from you.

I called Brown up yesterday, and found him home, so asked him if he had the book you spoke of, and asked if I could get it which he says sure, so I proceeded on down after it. Yes I have known Brown for some 12 or 14 years, I think I gave him most or the main part of his work in the Masonic lodge.

I find a lot or some names the same as in my uncles family, such as Wilson and Jay. My uncles name is John William Cissna who married my fathers sister, Mary Ann Clark. John William Cissna was born in Logan County, Illinois, November 13th, 1857, married January 22nd, 1879 in Council Bluffs, Pottawattamie County, Iowa. His father was Samuel Cissna and his mother's name was Mary Elizabeth Leach, who was born about the year 1830, died July 16th, 1903, where at I will have to find out later. He had brothers Samuel and Thomas that I know of and one sister Mary Ellen Cissna who married a great uncle of mine by name of Ellis Clark Jr. Mary Ann Clark was born February 28th, 1861 in Logan County, Illinois. Her fathers name, who is my grandfather, is John Jordon Clark 1835-1874 and her mother was Eliza Jane Houser, 1834-1876.

I would be very glad to have this family of Cissna's included in your genealogy, and I am sure that they would too. Soon as I can see some of them will show them "The House of Cessna" and tell them what you are going to do, and also I will try and get more records from uncle John, who his grandparents were, also all of his brothers and sisters and dates also. I have a lot of loose ends, that will have to be completed and then I will have them written up in some kind of shape, and maybe you can figure them out.

Most of the names I gave in the list in the Handbook are married into the Brobst's of which I suppose you have seen some records of them in your search, or probably know some of them. I have quite a lot of Brobst records, all with a lot of loose ends, but am having very good luck so far with this line.

Yours very truly,

L. A. Clark.

The House of Cessna

SPECIAL ATTENTION TO HEROES OF REVOLUTIONARY WAR IN '76.

———

Upon the suggestion of the United States George Washington Bi-centennial Commission that this Memorial Day would be an especially appropriate time to remember the patriots who died during the Revolutionary War, or who were surviving veterans of that conflict, patriotic societies and military organizations in Ross county moved today to include in the Memorial observance some specific recognition of the sacrifices of America's first veterans.

These men under General Washington battled with England's picked troops and won independence for the American people and it is felt by the Bi-centennial Commission that its suggested observance of Memorial Day will pay honor to Washington and all his soldiery.

The Daughters of American Revolution organization has listed several veterans of the War for Independence who are buried in Ross county cemetery. One of the best known graves in Chillicothe is that of Stephen Cissna, who is buried in Greenlawn. Cissna, a veteran of the Revolutionary War, came to Chillicothe from Bedford, Pa. Mrs. Peter J. Blosser, active member of the D. A. R., is acquainted with Cissna's descendants in Bedford and on their behalf decorates his grave every Memorial Day.

Mrs. Blosser stated that all graves of known Revolutionary War veterans would be appropriately decorated Memorial Day by some member of the D. A. R. organization.

DR. AND MRS. I. W. HOWERTH HONORED BY HUNDREDS ON THEIR GOLDEN WEDDING ANNIVERSARY AUGUST 16.

———

Festivities of their golden wedding anniversary were climaxed for Dr. and Mrs. I. W. Howerth Sunday evening, Aug. 15, by a banquet given in compliment to them by their faculty and town friends.

Dr. and Mrs. Howerth received friends during the day at their home, 1226 Tenth street, more than 300 students, townspeople and faculty associates calling on them. Students came at 9:30 a. m., calling at the home where they have spent many pleasant hours in informal social affairs. The reception continued through the day until 5:30 p. m.

Masses of gorgeous flowers transformed the house into a veritable garden. They, as well as numerous golden gifts on display, were sent by friends. Telegrams arrived during the day from Massachusetts, California and other places, friends unable to be present taking that means to send congratulations. Included in the gifts was $105 in gold, $50 having been sent from the faculty and $55 from the Howerth club and classes of Dr. Howerth, who is a professor of sociology at Colorado Teachers college and head of the department before his partial retirement this past year. The faculty also sent a gold wedding ring.

Pictures of Dr. and Mrs. Howerth were an interesting part of the reception. They showed them as children, on their wedding day wearing the formal costume of 50 years ago, and at various periods of their lives since. A book won by Mrs. Howerth, then Cora Cissna, when she was the young teacher's star pupil, was on display.

In the dining room, the table appointments carried out the golden color scheme, with golden glow arranged for the centerpiece and golden tapers shedding a soft glow in the room. Assisting there were Mrs. W. G. Binnewies, Mrs. Helen Spoelstra, Dorothy Clayton, Betty Blue, Ruth Binnewies and Minnie Lee.

At the close of their reception, Dr. and Mrs. Howerth were taken to the Faculty club, where 200 friends of the couple had gathered in their honor. Dinner was served in the dining room, the tables being decorated with golden flowers and lighted with ivory tapers.

Programs, printed in gold and carrying the wedding picture of Dr. and Mrs. Howerth, were at each place at the dinner.

Dr. W. S. Dando, formerly of Greeley and now pastor of the First Presbyterian church in Emporia, Kans., performed the second wedding ceremony, the "renewal of pledges," in the lounge of the club. Dr. Dando was visiting in Estes Park and was in Greeley for the week end.

The "bride," who renewed her vows of 50 years ago, was dressed in an Alice blue gown, matching the blue of her eyes. She wore a wedding veil, an ivory lace Cuban scarf mellowed with years, belonging to Mrs. David Kelly and the gift 20 years ago of her son, Ralph. The veil was caught into a hood of Duchesse lace and spray of orange blossoms loaned by Mrs. Ted Stockfleth, daughter of Mr. and Mrs. J. H. Shaw.

Joyce Perry as flower girl and Jane Frasier as ring bearer led the bridal procession. Miss Elizabeth Carney was maid of honor and Mrs. J. D. Heilman and Miss Rose Lammel were bridesmaids.

The bride entered on the arm of J. H. Shaw, and Dr. Frank Jean attended the groom.

June, 1931.

The first we knew of the Cissnas at Bellingham, Wash., came by the letter below. The attached copy of letter dated June 11, 1931 is in answer to one I wrote Ray C. Cissna a few weeks earlier.—Wanda Cessna.

Bellingham, Wash.
June 11, 1931.

Dear Miss Cessna: We are sorry to say we know none of the people you mention in your letter, however, we have made no effort to investigate our ancestry. Personally I would like to know something about it. The information I have is very remote and not taken from any written record.

My father tells me his father, whose name was also Charles, was born in Greenup County, Ohio, about 1820. His father, my grandfather—also Charles—was the son of one of three brothers who were soldiers in the army of Lafayette. The name might be found in records of the enlistment of Lafayette's army. They came from France to America in this way.

My grandfather had a family Bible in which there was

drawn a family crest and records were kept. The crest consisted of three brothers with clasped hands. A sort of Beau Geste gesture. My father was about seven years old when he saw it so it may have been only a game of hands. My grandfather who was a professional penman of some repute, had drawn in the crest himself. The Bible was lost in about 1867 when the family moved from Chesterton to Rancelier, Indiana.

My grandfather had two brothers: Robert and Samuel. Robert died without issue, Samuel went to the south west in about 1870 (when he was around 35). My father had four brothers: John, Robert, Will and Joe, now all deceased. His sister Anna is in Michigan. My father was born in Indiana in 1860. He has been an orphan since he was seven years old and has made his own way since that age. Ray and I are 48 and 24 respectively. We have no other brothers.

It is my contention that our spelling of the name, Cissna—came about through mistaking the French accent "grave" over the "e" for a dot over an "i."

Sorry we can't give you more information. We will be glad to hear from you again.

Yours very truly,

Chas. R. Cissna.

Wanda Cessna, Wichita, Kans.

July 18, 1930.

Mr. Cessna,

Cessna Aircraft Co.

Dear Sir: I am not interested in gliders though I did see your ad in magazine. What I am interested in is why you spell your name with an "E."

Three brothers, who spelled their name "Cissnaw," came over from France with Lafayette to help the colonies—heroes if you wish or just adventurous kids.

They stayed in this country dropping the "W" from the French name.

The House of Cessna

It so happens that my ancestors are almost pure French so I have the dark skin, the black hair and brown eyes of a Frenchman.

Very truly yours,
Ray C. Cissna.

These addresses were given me by my cousin, Mrs. J. F. Serowinsky, Venice, Calif.

C. C. Cessna, 564 Franklin, Whittier, Calif.
Mrs. Elvira J. Cesena, 735 S. Hope, Los Angeles.
N. W. Cessna, 358 S. Craig Ave., Pasadena, Calif.
H. J. Cessna, 6410 Makee, Los Angeles.
Sam Cessna, 1183 W. 39, Los Angeles.
Bernardette Cissna, 4262 W. 1st, Los Angeles.
Cliff R. Cissna, 708½ W. 41 Drive, Los Angeles.
Kenneth W. Cissna, 1729 W. 65 Place, Los Angeles.

CHAPTER XII

Captain Samuel T. Williams, a Descendant of
Squire James Cessna IV

613 McClellan Ave.,
Fort Leavenworth, Kansas.
July 16th, 1934.

Mr. Howard Cessna,
R. D. 4, Bedford, Pa.

My dear Sir: Your card of July 6th at hand.   I'm attaching hereto a check for $2.00 for your new Cessna Book.

In reference to our correspondence during the last winter, I got some data from my mother but have not had had the time to put it before you.   It is also attached hereto and I hope it is not too late to be included in your new addition. You undoubtedly have put a great deal of time and effort on this subject and deserve the thanks of all.   I wish your new book the greatest success.

Very truly yours,
Samuel T. Williams, Capt., Infantry, U. S. Army

(See Genealogical Table on p. 103)

The following is an outline of the Cessna branch that moved to Texas about 1870.

CHARLES, son of Squire JAMES by his second wife, moved to Urbana, Illinois, where as a result of desease contracted while a Union Soldier he died.   Prior to the Civil War he was twice married.

By his first marriage he had born to him two children: George and Mary Ellen.   GEORGE left the home in Illinois about 1870 to go to Texas.   He was never heard from again and his sisters think he met a violent death. MARY ELLEN married John Coffman and made their home in Chechalis, Wash., where she now lives (1934). Mary Ellen had two children: Harry, Jr. and Roy Coffman. These two boys married and each have two children. Harry remained in Chechalis and consolidated and advanced his father's business interests and at the time of his death in 1930 was a most prosperous and influential man. ROY is at present a dentist in Portland, Oregon.

The second wife of CHARLES was Mary Ann Dieber, born in Bedford in 1830, died at Denton, Texas, 1917. Of this second marriage there were three daughters: HENRIETTA, POLLY, and IDA.

HENRIETTA, born in 1853, died 1891. She fiirt married Hiram H. Bowman. One daughter was born, Opal who died in 1881. They moved to Texas in 1877. Mr. Bowman died in Feb. 1877. In 1880, Henrietta married Major David P. Smith, C.S.A., at Pittsburg, Texas. He died in August 1891. There had been no children by the second marriage.

POLLY, the second daughter, was born in 1885, died in 1918. Polly married Fred C. Clayton in 1876 and moved to Pittsburg, Texas, in 1877. She had five children as follows: Claude (no children), Will (no children), Paul (Paul, Jr. and Kathran), Elijah, and Annetta (Grady, Jr. and Kathran). Elijah moved to Elizabeth, N. J., which is his present home. The three other boys remained in Pittsburg, Texas, and are very successful business men in that community. Claude being among other things, Mayor of the city about fifteen years. The daughter, Annetta, married a Mr. Grady King of Dallas, Texas, their present home.

IDA, the third daughter, was born in Urbana, Ill. in 1859. She came to Texas with her sister Polly in 1877. Here she married Mr. Darwin Herbert Williams. Of this marriage there were six children as follows: Charles Swacy, Ed, Mary Mitchner, Ida, Samuel Tankersley, and Fred Cessna Williams. Mr. Williams died in 1918. IDA has made her home at Denton, Texas, since about 1900. Of her children CHARLES S. was born in 1882, he married Edith Malpas, children: Charles, Jr. and Lar-

CHARLES
son of
Sq. James
(2nd mar.)

George
(1st mar.)

Mary Ellen
(1st mar.) — Harry, Jr.
Roy

Henrietta
(2nd mar.) — Opal

Polly
(2nd mar.)
- Claude
- Will
- Paul — Paul, Jr.
Kathran
- Elijah
- Annetta — Grady, Jr.
Kathran

Ida
(2nd mar.)
- Charles S. — Larwin
Charles, Jr.
- Ed — Rachel Cessna
Ed Paxton
Linda Lee
- Mary M. — Woodson Herbert
Richard Alexander
Ida Ann
- Ida — Mary Annetta
Charles Williams
Samuel James
Mercer Lenor
- Samuel
Tankersley
- Fred Cessna — Alfred
Miltilda

The House of Cessna

win. Present home, La Oroya, Peru, South America, where he is Supt. of Power of the Cerro de Pasco Copper Corporation. ED was born in 1885, he married Sophie Cochran. Children: Ed Paxton, Rachel Cessna, and Linda Lee. Present home is at Fort Worth, Texas, where he is Director of Public Schools. MARY MITCHNER was born in 1890, married Mr. Woodson A. Harris. Children: Woodson Herbert, Richard Alexander, and Ida Ann. Present home is at Denton, Texas, where Mr. Harris and sons are in business, groceries, real estate and ranching. IDA, born in 1893, married Mr. Mercer Lenor Henderson. Children: Mary Annetta, Charles Williams, Samuel James and Mercer Lenor Henderson, Jr. Present home, Denton, Texas. Mr. Henderson, prior to his death in 1920 was a cotton broker. SAMUEL TANKERSLEY, born in 1897, married Jewel Charlott Spear of Little Rock, Arkansas. (No children). Officer in the Regular Army. FRED CESSNA, born 1902. Married Viola Gillis. Children: Alfred and Miltilda. At present in business in Denton, Texas.

CHAPTER XIII

Descendants of Several Branches of the Cessna Family

DESCENDANTS OF RACHEL CESSNA WILLIAMS

The following was given me by Mrs. Sarah Rose Gump, Everett.

Henry William married Rachel Cessna, daughter of Major John Cessna, March 20, 1781.

Issue: Hannah, born May 24, 1782; John, born August 30, 1784; Sarah, born July 1, 1786; Margaret, born February 25, 1789; Elizabeth, born April 12, 1791; Rebeckah, born March 4, 1794; Rachel, born April 9, 1797; May, born March 11, 1800.

Rachel married Edmund McCoy.

Issue: Susannah, Jackson, Henry, Frank. Dr. Walter McCoy received medal for ability shown in research work.

Sarah married Samuel Smith.

Issue: William, born December 3, 1808; Hannah, born May 20, 1811; Anthony, born December 13, 1813; Henry, born August 3, 1816.

Henry Smith married Susannah McCoy, Feb. 1843.

Issue: Emily V., born Dec. 11, 1844, married M. W. Clippinger, she died April 24, 1883, and he died May 2, 1883. Barton Cooper, born Dec. 28, 1845, married Laura L. Case, Oct. 11, 1870. Hannah Marden, born April 6, 1847, married Wilson Evans, Dec 25, 1876, died Nov. 24, 1877. Louise A., born Jan. 8, 1849, married George W. Williams, Sept. 14, 1870. Osborn W., born Sept. 23, 1850. Edmond McCoy, born March 17, 1852, married Sarah B. McClelland, Oct. 12, 1875. Sarah Rose, born June 24, 1853, married Sidney Gump, Dec. 5, 1877. Rachel, born Aug. 13, 1855, married David W. Lee, Nov. 28, 1900. David Lee died May 1, 1910. Jennie E., born March 23, 1857, married Rev. John Leilick, Sept. 29, 1880, died March 31, 1883. Annabel, born March 18, 1859, married Rev. H. L. El-

The House of Cessna

derdice, June 3, 1881 or 1891.   Myra O. Smith, born April 28, 1861.

Henry Smith died Feb. 15, 1899, Susannah Smith died May 1, 1909.

John Cessna married Sarah Rose, Jan. 26, 1760.   They were born near Shippensburg, Penna., and moved to Bedford County about 1765.

DESCENDANTS OF SARAH CESSNA JAMES

Descendants of Sarah Cessna James.   Sarah Cessna was a granddaughter of Major John Cessna.

George James was born 1782.   Sarah Cessna James was born May 6, 1788.

Their children: John James, born Nov. 7, 1806; Jeremiah James, born Oct. 15, 1808; Anna James, born May 6, 1811; William James, born Aug. 19, 1813; Rachel James, born Sept. 11, 1815; Geo. W. James, born March 17, 1818; Samuel James, born May 20, 1820; Alexander James, born June 18, 1822; Mary Ellen James, born Oct. 1, 1824; Sarah Elizabeth James, born May 24, 1827; Geo. W. James, born Dec. 20, 1830; Margaret James, born March 18, 1834.

DESCENDANTS OF CHARLES CESSNA IV, A SON OF MAJ. JOHN CESSNA

Mr. Howard Cessna,
    Attorney at Law,
        Bedford, Pennsylvania.

Dear Cousin: This will acknowledge receipt of your letter of the 4th, instant, with reference to your history of the Cessna family.

Following is the family of John Cessna, son of Charles Cessna IV. John Cessna was born March 14, 1817 and died Nov. 21, 1893. His first wife was Sarah Nartin. Nine children as follows: Nancy, died when a child; Catherine, dead, never married; Katura, dead; George, dead; Annie, dead; William, dead; Liza, dead; Mary, died in early childhood; Sara, died in early childhood.

The family of Katura, first marriage, Mrs. Ogden, two children, Mary and Christina.

Katura, second marriage, Mrs. R. Shaffner, three children, Edith, Carrie and Eliza.

The family of George Cessna, first marriage to Melissa Davis, ten children as follows: Bell, John, Richard, Barton, George, Anna, Edith, Molly, Dolly and Sarah.

George Cessna, second marriage to Laura Ginter, four children as follows: Lloyd, William, Allien and James.

Anna Cessna, married to Thomas Nichols, two children: Fanny and Bessie.

William Cessna, first marriage to Martha Coy, five children as follows: Blair, Earl, Frank, May and Charles.

William Cessna, second marriage to Jennie Coy, five children as follows: Ida, Grace, Melissa, Cota and Dillie.

Eliza Cessna, married to Joseph Coy, two children, Verdie and Omah.

John Cessna, second wife, Abagail Jane Keslar, six children, Ada, Milton, Ida, Lilly, Mildred and Malissa.

Ada, married to Thomas Hickox, three children as follows: Elsie, Bessie and Edgar.

Milton, married to Martha Bowers, twelve children as follows: Harcey, Clyde, Quay, Glenn, John, Ellen, Arthur, Marie, Wayne, Lilly May, Lila June, and Jacob.

Ida, married to A. M. Tyger, six children as follows: Ralph, Otto, Oakley, Isaac Ray, Clair and Carl.

Lilly, married to H. G. Bowers, three children as follows: I. Ray, Frank and Paul.

Mildred, married to C. H. Tyger, two children, Gladys and Olive.

Melissa E. (Cessna) McCall, married to A. F. McCall, four children, Margaret Jane, Franklin Blair, Milton Cessna, and Howard Ray.

Margaret and Blair died when children, Milton Cessna McCall, married to Blanche Demott, no children. Milton is a grad-

The House of Cessna

uate of Pennsylvania State College, in the School of Mining and Engineering, is employed in the United States Bureau of Mines.

Howard, married to Earla Jane Gourley, two children, Frank Earle McCall and William Milton McCall. Howard is a graduate of the University of Pittsburgh, Dental School, and is practicing Dentistry in Punxsutawney.

Trusting this information will meet with your approval, I am,

> Sincerely yours,
> Mrs. A. F. McCall,
> 702 East Mahoning Street,
> Punxsutawney, Pa.

RALPH W. CESSNA OF THE CHRISTIAN SCIENCE MONITOR

August 27, 1934.

Howard Cessna,
R. D. 4, Bedford, Pa.

Dear Cousin: Your card went first to "Any Cessna" in Battle Creek, Mich., then to the same in Albion, where it was delivered to my mother, Mrs. O. J. Cessna. She then sent it on to me. Hence the delay in replying.

I am particularly anxious to have the book for my three year old son, Dana Jay, who is named after a cousin, Dana D. Beardslee, on my mother's side of the family, and my father, Otis Jay Cessna. My father, by the way, in case you are still compiling family data, passed on at Albion, Aug. 6, 1933. It also occurs to me that you might be interested in my wife's name. She was Fannie A. Adolphson, daughter of Mr. and Mrs. Gustav A. Adolphson, natives of Sweden, now residing in Arlington, Mass.

I have been connected with the Monitor for five years and next month go to take charge of our bureau in Chicago. Please send the book to me in care of the Central Bureau, Christian Science Monitor, 333 Michigan Ave., Chicago.

I recently read an article in some paper from Pennsylvania about "Uncle John" Cessna. I suppose the book will tell more about him. I would be interested to hear from you about Cessna family matters if you care to write.

Sincerely,

Ralph W. Cessna.

W. BROWNE CESSNA OF COUNCIL BLUFFS, IOWA

June 18, 1934.

Hon. Howard Cessna,
 Bedford, Pennsylvania.

Dear Howard: Loren Clark of Council Bluffs was up to my house yesterday and returned the book of "The House of Cessna's" that he had borrowed. He was telling me that you are getting up a new book or an addition to the old one. If this is a fact I can give you the following data that you might be able to use:

Descendants of W. B. Cessna and Ida Smith Cessna:

Albert Boone Cessna born Aug. 18, 1908. Died at childbirth.

Virginia Cessna Peterson, born Oct. 13, 1909. Her issue: Patsy Ruth Peterson, born March 13, 1929; Browne Cessna Peterson, born Nov. 10, 1932.

Wife of W. Browne Cessna born Nov. 26, 1872, married Dec. 25, 1899.

Now if it would do any good, as I understand it might in the way of selling the books, I can get you the history of my wife's immediate family, dates, etc. I expect to be in Sioux City tomorrow evening and will call on Mr. Andy Jackson. He is a cousin of ours that you know. Let me hear from you sometime as to what you are doing in regard to this work.

Ida joins me in best regards to yourself and wife.

I was down and saw my mother a week ago yesterday, and Saturday. She was 91 last Tuesday and is keeping up pretty good.

Yours truly,

W. Browne Cessna.

CLYDE M. CESSNA, RAPID CITY, SOUTH DAKOTA

July 16, 1934.

Howard Cessna,
  R. D. 4, Bedford, Pa.

Dear Cousin: This A. M. I received your card stating that you were planning on putting out another Book. I have "The House of Cessna" and I would not take any amount for it.

I am the youngest son of the John Cessna Tree. Have two older sisters living and one brother, Ed. Have lost two brothers within the last few years.

I was the only one of the boys that raised my children. I have two sons: James Edward Cessna, age 25, who is now a teacher in the public schools here; Clinton Clyde Cessna, age 23, who is a Mining Engineer and has charge of the Maywood Chemical Mines here.

Last summer I had the pleasure of meeting Paul Cessna and wife from Gettysburg, Pa., while they were touring the Black Hills, and they sure were real people.

Am sorry that you could not all be with us this year as we have hundreds of thousands of tourists here this year. We have a special attraction this year as the Geographic Society and the Government are sending up the largest balloon ever built. They expect to take off Thursday of this week.

Should you ever make a trip West don't fail to take in the Black Hills.

Sincerely,
Clyde M. Cessna.

ARLEE G. CISNEY, NEHAWHA, NEBRASKA

Nehawka, Nebr., Oct. 16, 1934.

Mr. Howard Cessna,

Dear Sir: Enclosed you will find a record of my father's family, as in talking to Wm. Browne Cessna, he told me you were working on a new edition. Wm. B. also said your price would be $2.00, so am enclosing that amount, also and wish my order placed for one copy.

In 1918 I had the pleasure of talking to you a few moments over the phone from Bedford and was sorry I didn't get to see you, was treated fine though by the ones I met that evening and will always remember them.

We are in the midst of the worst drouth in the history of the country here. Our corn will hardly make anything but fodder. We are used to 40 or 60 bushels per acre and when we come down to 2 to 4 and 5 bushels per acre, you know that is nothing. We are glad of a few late showers that brought up our wheat and pastures are greening up again so I guess everything will come out all right.

How are crop conditions with you folks? Fine I hope.

Well I will not bother you more and thanking you for the bother, I am,

> Yours truly,
>
> Arlee G. Cisney (Mike)
> Nehawka, Nebr.

STEPHEN SYLVESTER CISNEY, grandson of Stephen Cessna V. Born Jan. 4, 1857, occupation farmer, married Feb. 23, 1879 to Miss Marjorie J. Stephens of Newark, Indiana.

Issue: Earl L. Cisney, Odessa P., Stephen Sydney, Inez Maude, Arlee Glenn (Mike), Joseph Allen, Ernest Randolph, Kinley John.

EARL L. CISNEY. Born Oct. 11, 1880, occupation farmer, married Dec. 27, 1915 to Pearl L. Sherer, at Coleridge, Nebr.

Issue: Lawerence E., Shirley Mae, Hazel M., Warren G., Weldon E., Avis I.

ODESSA PEARL CISNEY. Born June 19, 1883, married Wil-

STEPHEN SYDNEY CISNEY. Born May 19, 1885, occupation, officer of the Law.

Issue: Ross M., Glenn A., Faye L., Leafa V., Zelma L., Orville E., William L., Jr.

The House of Cessna

Glenn A. Roberts. Born Sept. 18, 1906, occupation, Oil Company Operator, married Ester Smith, March 18, 1926.

Issue: Gene W., Richard D.

Second marriage 1930 to Stella J. Cookman in North Dakota. Issue: Glenna Rae, and Gay Lafaye.

Faye L. Roberts. Born May 29, 1908, occupation, Highway Engineer, married Evelyn Ericson, 1931 at Elkpoint, South Dakota. No issue.

Leafa V. Roberts. Born Jan. 18, 1910, married Muril J. Kiser, September 26, 1930.

Issue: Joan Patricia, and Muril Lee.

STEPHEN SYDNEY CISNEY. Born May 19, 1885, occupation farmer, married Feb. 23, 1904 to Emma Jane Henderson at Coleridge, Nebr.

Issue: Stephen S., Leslie M., R. Grace, S. Giles, D. Bruce.

Stephen Sylvester Cisney. Born Nov. 17, 1904, married Eda P. Dupree, May 25, 1929 in Los Angeles.

Issue: Ronald E.

Leslie Merril Cisney. Born June 2, 1907, married, May 18, 1925 to Helen Ima Hight at Yankton, South Dakota.

Issue: Phyllis E., Paul D., Francis I., Douglas D.

Ruby Grace Cisney. Born July 13, 1911, married, Feb. 11, 1931 to Roy Blenton Anberson.

Issue: Darrell E., Maurice D.

INEZ MAUDE CISNEY. Born Feb. 22, 1887, married Fred C. Gibson, March 20, 1907 at Coleridge, Nebr., occupation, farmer.

Issue: Marjorie C., A. Eunice, Wilfred C., Nina V. G., Berniece W., Arlene A., Keith E., James F. G., Floyd S., L. Eugene.

Marjorie C. Gibson. Born March 4, 1908, married James Collison, June 26, 1929 at Cherokee, Iowa. No issue.

Wilfred C. Gibson. Born March 12, 1912, married Esther Nixon, October 21, 1933 at Onawa, Iowa.

Issue: Eunice Irene, Sept. 23, 1934.

Berniece W. Gibson. Born Sept. 6, 1916, married Dale A. Brown, March 10, 1934 at South Sioux City, Nebr. No issue.

ARLEE GLENN CISNEY (Mike). Born April 16, 1889, occupation, farmer, married Vianna Pearl Lewis, March 20, 1911 at Coleridge, Nebr.

Issue: Don Lewis and Dean Lewis (twins), died in infancy, Wilma Maurine, Richard Dale, Robbie Glenn.

Army record, Private Company E, 10th Motor Supply Train.

JOSEPH ALLEN CISNEY. Born Sept. 9, 1882, occupation, farmer, married Ruby Mae Hanham, Feb. 25, 1915.

Issue: Doyle E., Thelma L., Merle E., Blanche V., Claire E., Kenneth E.

ERNEST RANDOLPH CISNEY. Born May 18, 1894, occupation, mechanic. Army record, Private, Company A. 341 Machine Gun Battalion 89th Division. Not married.

KINLEY JOHN CISNEY. Born May 22, 1896, occupation, farmer, married Imo Mae Olsen, May 26, 1920 at Coleridge, Nebr.

Issue: Betty Jean, died in infancy, Gordon D.

Army record, enlisted April 25, 1917. Served Battery B. first Anti Air Craft Battalion C. A. C., A. E. F. Served 7 months in United States and 15 months over seas.

PERMITTING JOINING COLONIAL DAMES

Santa Barbara, Calif., April 13, 1928.

Mr. Howard Cessna,
    Attorney at Law,
        Bedford, Pa.

Dear Friend: Mrs. Smith and Eleanor have been admitted to the D. A. R. as descendants of Major John Cessna, due largely to the assistance of yourself in furnishing desired information.

They have now been asked to join the local Chapter of Daughters of the Early American Colonists, which requires ancestral descent of at least one or more generations prior to the Revolution. I understand that the first John Cessna came to this country in 1690. The name of his wife is required; the name of his children and their wives or husbands, and other information. I believe that this information is contained in your

The House of Cessna

book, "The House of Cessna." If you have a copy to spare send it to me together with bill for same and I will be pleased to remit. If you have no extra copy, kindly loan me a copy, which I will immediately return.

The information required is where the ancestors of Major John Cessna lived, what they did, when they were born and died, together with a record of their marriages, and what part they played in the development of the country in which they lived.

Thanking you for this information, I am,

Very truly yours,

Oscar W. Smith.

Answer: John Cesna, Ensign, 1747-48, Pa. Arch. 2nd series, p. 511, also Judges of Common Pleas, Pa. Arch. 2nd series, vol. III, p. 764. This early service permits Cessna's joining Colonial Organizations, Ed.

Asking for Information

Ravenswood, W. Va., Dec. 10, 1927.

Bedford County Historical Society,
Bedford, Pennsylvania.

Gentlemen: Will you send me the following:

1. The correct date of marriage of Stephen Cisne (Cessna), who was born April 17, 1782 and died June 2, 1829 and his wife Mary Rose, born March 3, 1787 and died in 1829.

2. The correct date of birth of Emanuel Cisne (Cessna), who was the son of Stephen and Mary (Rose) Cisne.

I will appreciate the above information at your earliest convenience and any expense incurred will be paid upon receipt of data.

Thanking you, I am sincerely,

Mrs. L. T. Thorn.

2424 Park Ave., Minneapolis, Minn.

Mr. Howard Cessna,
  Bedford, Pennsylvania

Dear Mr. Cessna: I notice in "Who's Who in Genealogy" that you have compiled a genealogy of the Cessna family.

Eleanor Cisne (Cessna) born 1804, died Sept. 25, 1867, daughter of Stephen Cisne of Perry County, Pa., was married after 1824 to John McKeehan of Cumberland County. In 1844 John McKeehan moved with his family to a farm near Larwill, Whitney County, Indiana, and thus more or less severed connections with eastern relatives.

Have you the line of Stephen Cisne (Cessna) in your book and can you tell me of any library in this part of the country from which I could borrow it? I am very desirous of finding the line of Stephen back to John Cessna of France from whom he was descended.

Any help you can give me will be most gratefully appreciated.

Very truly yours,

Aug. 14, 1932.   Mrs. George P. Douglas.

THEOPHOLUS CISNEY'S DESCENDANTS

A more complete list of descendants of W. Henry Cisney V, Thomas IV, Theopholus III, as shown in "House of Cessna," page 116.

Wm. Henry Cisney V married Margaret Kelly, he died 1932, and his wife died 1908.

Issue: Sarah Jane, Alfred John, George W., Elizabeth, Lucy, Thomas Emmert.

Sarah Jane VI, married Sharswood Parsons, 1405 Center St., Wilkinsburg, Pa.

Issue: Russel, M.D., died in France, 1918; Ruth, Musical Director in schools at Pittsburgh, Pa.; Esther, Elmer, Franklin, lawyer, lives in Coral Gables, Miami, Fla., and Sarah.

Alfred John VI, married Lyda Maud Pipes. He was born 1871 ,died 1926; wife born 1879.

Issue: William Rufus, born 1900; Gladys, born 1902, married Frederick D. Trismen, who have a daughter, Maud, born 1931. Address: Buck Hill Falls, Pa. Luella born 1905, married Joel K. Skidmore. Issue: Joel Alfred born 1929 and Sally Lue, born 1933.

George W. Cisney VI, married Anna.

Issue: Samuel, Lenore.

Address, Merrich Road, Springfield, L. I.

Elizabeth Cisney VI, married Edwin A. Smith, both medical doctors.

Issue: Edwin Junior, Margaret.

Address, 319 Park Avenue, Warren, Ohio.

Lucy Cisney VI, married Allen Kauffman.

Issue: Georgia, Margaret, lived in Harrisburg, Pa.

Thomas Cisney VI, married Stella.

Issue: Emmert, Bert, Kenneth.

Address, Brooklyn, N. Y.

LETTER FROM CISNE, ILLINOIS

Cisne, Ill., Aug. 9, 1934.

Dear Cousin: Your card regarding the Cessna Book received, have been slow in answering.

I had four brothers and four sisters. Now I have just two brothers and one sister living. Sister is seventy-six last October, is in poor health just now. She suffered a paralytic stroke last fall. One sister died last November with paralysis.

I am seventy-four years old. I have just one daughter. We live together in Cisne, her husband is Maintenance Patrolman.

Hoping you and yours are well,

Cousin, Sarah J. Stine.

ELLEN CESSNA JACKSON RECORD AND ELEANOR CESSNA GASTON'S DESCENDANTS

Sioux City, Iowa, May 15, 1932.

Mr. Howard Cessna,
 Lutzville, Bedford Co., Pa.

Dear Mr. Cessna: I am deeply appreciative of your kindness in having loaned me the Cessna pamphlet. I am returning it with this letter. May I ask you to keep me in mind and if another copy is at sometime available I would be grateful to have one.

I note with interest that our James Jackson was a Cessna. I thought you might like to have for your family scrap book the enclosed clippings concerning Mr. Jackson, and his daughter who married Dr. John K. Cook. A son is living here now and is one of my best friends.

Your reference to "Forts of Pennsylvania" is most tantalizing. You know spaces out here in the middle west are broad and Sioux City is at the corner of three states whose libraries are all long miles distant. Another point which may surprise you is that until your letter I had not the least conception of the conditions in Bedford county at the time of the Revolution. Out here our Revolutionary data is confined to what is to be gleaned from United States Histories, and even the best of them have very little space except for the struggle along the eastern seaboard. I can readily see that your mind is a storehouse of historical lore, and it is probably hard for you to realize the utter ignorance of some one like myself. You have been so gracious that I am hoping you can find time to answer a few questions for me:

a. Do you think Evan Cessna served under his brother "John?"

b. Do you think Evan Cessna was present with his company at Valley Forge?

c. Just what would a company of Frontier Rangers under Evan Cessna, Captain, be doing?

In your pamphlet you speak names which are like doors to

which I have no keys, Christopher Gist, Col. Armstrong, Chief Wills, Chief Rains. Oh, don't misunderstand me, I am not asking you to give me a course in Bedford County history, but if you will just write me a paragraph or two I will be grateful.

Thank you again for the courtesy of the letter and for the loan of the pamphlet.

Sincerely,
Gertrude Henderson,

(I appreciate this letter, Ed).

ELEANOR CESSNA RECORD

Cambridge, Ohio, Aug. 2, 1934.

Mr. Howard Cessna,
  Bedford, Pennsylvania.

Dear Cousin: I am mailing with this letter the history I have hurriedly collected of Ellen Cessna Jackson to be compiled in the new Cessna Book. I have made a rough chart similar to the ones used in the last book you published. Am also sending the material sent me by my relatives. It includes a short sketch of Ellen Jackson's life and family. Use of it what you think necessary. I'm also enclosing my check for $2.00 and think a number of others in the family will want the book. I am enclosing a list of my relatives and their addresses. If you would drop them a card they doubtless would be interested. A number of us are members of D. A. R., and others might become members if they knew of the Cessna line and of the ancestors who served so bravely in the Revolutionary War. I hope sometime when I drive through Pennsylvania to drop in for a call with you and hope you will not pass us by if you journey through Cambridge, which is on the Main Street of America, the old National Road, National Highway No. 40.

With kindest regards, I am,

Yours truly,
Mergeline Shriver Boyd.

Mrs. A. W. Boyd,
   622 N. 7th St., Cambridge, Ohio.

Ellen Caroline Jackson and her husband Alexander Record left Oregon, Missouri with their large family in 1862. After the privitations of the Civil War had dwindled their blooded stock and their lives were threatened by the Kansas Jay Hawkers. They moved to Council Bluffs, Iowa, where her brother James Jackson, had an Indian trading store. Her son William established a small tin shop, soon after their arrival, at the age of twelve years. Her son James drove an oxen team from Missouri by himself, passing through Glenwood, Iowa, where the family later located, buying a farm in 1869, one mile north of town on what is now National Highway, No. 34, where a home was maintained until after her husband's death in 1900.

Her son James later bought the farm across the road from the home and put in a large orchard. This farm was held by his daughter, Janet, until 1931, when it was sold for a Country and Golf Club. Her sons, Samuel and Charles, also owned farms adjoining the home place for many years, but these too have now passed out of the family. Her son James and her son-in-law, Russell Thompson, sold the first Singer Sewing Machines, and first Organs in the County of Mills. Her daughter Mary Jane (Mrs. Shriver), taught one of the first schools in the County.

Few of the descendants of Ellen Jackson Record now reside near the old home. One son, Charles, only of her large family, is still living. He resides with his wife in Glenwood, near the old home. His daughter, Verna Johnson, and her family, reside nearby on a farm.

Janet Pike (James' daughter) still lives with her husband in Glenwood, as does also Elsa Jones (Ada's daughter). The rest of the family descendants are scattered from coast to coast.

HISTORY OF RACHEL CESSNA JACKSON'S CHILD,
ELEANOR CAROLINE JACKSON

Eleanor Caroline Jackson, born Dec. 28, 1824, died Dec. 12,

1905, married Alexander Record in Holt County, Missouri, Sept. 10, 1840.

Children: Andrew J., born July 16, 1841, died Feb. 6, 1867; Julia Ann, born Oct. 3, 1842, died, 1919; John A., born Feb. 29, 1844, died Oct. 19, 1845; William L., born March 4, 1846, died, 1915; James F., born March 31, 1848, died July 19, 1914; Robert W., born Dec. 19, 1849, died April 16, 1882; Mary Jane, born Dec. 29, 1851, died March 3, 1930; Margaret Henrietta, born Dec. 6, 1853, died April 25, 1889; Samuel B., born June 26, 1856, died Jan. 2, 1913; Charles H., born March 27, 1859, died; Rachel Eleanor, born May 4, 1861, died Feb. 1, 1863; Ida H., born Sept. 7, 1863, died Oct. 3, 1865; Ada, born Feb. 19, 1866, died March 13, 1902.

Alexander Record husband of Eleanor Caroline Jackson, born March 3, 1817, died Sept. 29, 1900.
March 3, 1817, died Sept. 29, 1900.

History of: Julia Ann Record, born Oct. 3, 1842, died in the year 1919, married G. R. Thompson.

Children: Geo. A. Thompson, March 9, 1878; John Thompson, Feb. 29, 1880; Maggie Thompson, Oct., 1884.

George A. Thompson married Nell Gilbrath, Dec. 19, 1895. Los Angeles, Calif.

John Thompson married Daisy —— who had the following children: Robert, Russel, John (deceased), Raymond (deceased), Arthur, Daisy Mae and William. Fullerton, Calif.

Maggie Thompson, married first time to Karl Weaver, and second time to B. O. King. One son to first marriage, Paul Weaver. Los Angeles, Calif.

History of: William L. Record, born March 4, 1846, died in the year 1915. Married Tillie McKelvy.

Children: Ida Record Fabing (all deceased). Oakland, Calif.

History of: James Franklin Record, born March 31, 1848, died July 19, 1914. Married Sarah E. Williams, (deceased).

Children: Janet, born March 11, 1880; Eleanor May, born May, 1882, (deceased). Janet married Harry L. Pike, Dec. 14, 1909. Glenwood, Iowa.

History of: Mary Jane Record, always called Jennie, born

Dec. 29, 1851, died March 3, 1930. Married Dr. Frances M. Shriver, Nov. 11, 1874.

Children: Mergeline Elizabeth, married Dr. A. W. Boyd, Cambridge, Ohio.

Dr. Shriver, born in 1845, still living at 89 years, and in good health.

History of: Margaret H. Record, born Dec. 6, 1853, died April 25, 1889. Married M. G. Edwards, Nov. 11, 1874.

Children: Dr. J. Arch Edwards, born Aug. 11, 1874. Oakdale, Iowa.

Charles W. Edwards, born Feb. 2, 1876, married Carrie Cook, Feb. 5, 1908, have two children, Elizabeth and Milton.

Elizabeth, married Harold Workman, have two children, Charles and Stanley. Iowa City, Iowa.

Mable Edwards, born Oct. 30, 1887, died Jan., 1924, married J. M. Mollett, have two children, Dorothy, born Feb. 20, 1914, and Charmian, born Nov., 1920. Los Angeles, Calif.

History of: Samuel B. Record, born Oregon, Missouri, June 26, 1856, died Jan. 2, 1913. Married Lora B. Moon, Sept. 3, 1889, Glenwood, Iowa.

Children: Lucile, born Oct. 16, 1892; Franklin A., born Aug. 25, 1895; Helen Eleanor, born Oct. 28, 1897.

Lucile Record married Frank Hunt, Dec. 19, 1915, have three children: Halliette Helen, born Sept. 2, 1918; James Franklin, born Jan. 16, 1921; Richard Record, born April 21, 1926. San Bernardino, Calif.

Franklin A. Record, unmarried. Colton, Calif.

Helen Record married Chas. McGready. Ontario, Calif.

History of: Charles H. Record, born Oregon, Missouri, March 27, 1859. Married Rose M. Bachman, Dec. 17, 1884, at Shelton, Nebraska.

Children: Verna Eleanor, born Jan. 19, 1888; Corinne Bonfoy, born Sept. 7, 1893; Edna Mae, born Jan. 5, 1897; Robert Warner, born Jan. 5, 1902.

Verna Record married John W. Johnson, Dec. 14, 1912, have one daughter, Rachel Rose, born May 5, 1916. Glenwood, Iowa.

The House of Cessna

Corinne B. Record, married Karl J. Knoepflet, Sept. 19, 1916, have three children: Robert John, born Jan. 15, 1919; James Charles born Nov. 18, 1921; Donald Wilson born Sept. 18, 1931. Sioux City, Iowa.

Edna Record married Duane S. Kidder, Nov. 29, 1927, Sioux City, Iowa.

Robert W. Record, Chicago, Ill.

History of: Ada Record, born Feb. 19, 1866, died March 13, 1902. Married Jos. H. Ewing, Oct. 26, 1886.

Children: Elsa, born July 23, 1887.

Elsa Ewing, married Clarence L. Jones, Oct. 21, 1908, have two children: Ewing L., born April 23, 1912, and Janet E., born May 11, 1915. Glenwood, Iowa.

Present address of following:

Mrs. Frank Hunt, Box 845, Rt. 2, San Bernardino, Calif.

Mrs. B. O. King, 3243 East Anaheim St., Long Beach, Calif.

Mrs. Karl Knoepfler, 30 Blackstone Ave., Sioux City, Iowa.

Dr. James A. Edwards, Oakdale, Iowa.

Mr. Andrew Jackson, Sioux City, Iowa.

Mr. C. H. Record, Glenwood, Iowa.

Mrs. H. L. Pike, Glenwood, Iowa.

Venice, Calif.

Dear Cousin Howard: I am glad to know you are going to print a new book and hope you will see fit to have my grandmother's branch or limb of the tree attached. If you do, I will tell you the correct spelling for the names:

Eleanor Cessna married Rev. Gaston, who had the following children: Josiah Cessna Gaston and James Cessna Gaston.

Eleanor Cessna married the second time to Thos. C. McGavran, who had the following children: Dr. John Cessna McGavran; Sarah Ellen McGavran Woolman, Helena, Mont.; Josephine McGavran Jack, Butte, Mont.; Janette McGavran Kinna, Butte, Mont.; Thomas Walter McGavran, Los Angeles, Calif., who married and had the following children: Marguerite McGavran and Clarence Henry McGavran.

Marguerite McGavran married ——— Serowinsky, and had two children: Frances Marie Serowinsky McCardle and Jack Joseph Serowinsky.

Clarence H. McGavran married ———, had two children: Clarence McGavran and Florence McGavran.

Your Cousin,

Marguerite Cessna Serowinsky.

CLARA CESSNA ERHARD, DAUGHTER OF JACOB S. CESSNA VI—
(See House of Cessna page 91)

Aug. 26, 1934.

Dear Cousin: Brother Charles' wife called me about three weeks ago to tell me about your card concerning the new book you are having published. I meant to help her write for him and order one for myself, but something else claimed my attention at the time and I just learned a day or two ago when I returned from a trip that she had not written. Charlie suffered a stroke last November and while much improved, able to walk with assistance, his hand is still helpless so that he cannot write.

Many changes have taken place since last I saw you—no doubt you'd fail to recognize the gray-haired grandmother. Am wondering what there is to your account genealogically.

I presume you have all your data compiled and sent to the publishers, but because of your interest in the various "twigs" will give you a short sketch of both Charlies life and mine since leaving Bedford County. He has been in the employ of the B. & O. R. R., as ticket agent at Johnstown, Smithfield, Uniontown, and Connellsville, consecutively. In August 1909, at Smithfield, he married Blanche Leech, who died in Sept. 1910, leaving a baby girl, Frances. He came here in 1920 but was transferred to the office in Connellsville two years ago. Jan. 1916, he married Miss Ethel Brown, this city. He owns his home, and Frances, who is still single, at home, will teach her fourth term in the city schools. His wife was a nurse, so he is very fortunate in having such care in his affliction.

The House of Cessna

As for myself, I presume you remember when I married J. Grant Jamison, Feb. 22, 1989. Our only daughter, Mary Lyndall, was born Feb. 20, 1902. He died July 20, 1903. I married J. Addison Erhard Aug. 6, 1907, at Hyndman, and he died at Glassport, Feb. 15, 1913, during his fifth term as principal of the schools there. From that time till Charles' marriage, I kept house for him—mother was also with us till her death in 1920. My daughter was married in October, 1925 to Berwyn S. Detweiler, who is in the automobile business. They have four children, so "grandma" is kept busy. We live at 234 Wilson Ave., and would be very glad to have you call any time you chance to be near and I'm sure Charles would be also—his wife expressed a desire to meet you.

Enclosed you will find $4.00 to pay for a book for each of us, I often regretted not having one of the others.

Wishing you success in your undertaking and with kindest regards, I remain your cousin,

Clara V. Erhard.

P. S. Presume you have all available data concerning the history of the planting of the family "tree" in this country, but thought I might mention that Charles is proud of the possession of a copied reference to a Jean de Cessna who came from Ireland in 1740, taken from Memoirs of the Huguenots.

C. V. E.

LOUISE HUMMER, DAUGHTER OF WEAVER B. CESSNA VI—
(*See House of Cessna page 67*)

Latrobe, Sept. 12, 1934.

Dear Cousin Howard: Pardon my delay in forwarding to you the information regarding our family—also the copy of your address before the Western Historical Society—I enjoyed reading it and was tempted to keep it for my scrap book only that I promised to return it.

Names and dates in first paragraph of our family history

page 67 of "House of Cessna," are correct so far as I know except my birth date is Aug. 15, 1883, and my brother Dow, Aug. 2, 1885.

1. Frances Eugenia Cessna, deceased. One, name Gladys.

2. Eldesta Idella Cessna.

3. Florence Evelyn Cessna. One, name Olive.

4. Stephen Douglas Cessna.

5. Charles Carroll Cessna, deceased. Names of children: Bernadine and Anna Zeta.

6. John Snowden Cessna. Occupation, real estate business.

7. Mary Rosamond Cessna, Saxton, Pa. Married J. Martin Fink. Issue: Walter, Roxie Maud, Zella, Ora, Claudia.

8. Joseph Howard Cessna, Bedford, Pa., R. D. No. 2, farmer, married Jennie Crawford. Issue: Charles, Margaret, John, Louise, Mary Anna, Billy.

9. Clara Violet Cessna, deceased, Saxton, Pa., married Phil. A. Barnett, manufacturer. Issue: Eugene, Will.

10. Anna Myrtle Cessna, Marysville, Pa., married Dr. H. O. Lightner. Issue: Linn, Joe, Donald.

11. Ethel Grame Cessna, Pittsburgh, Pa., married J. B. Lobingier. Issue: Louise, Helena, Ethel, Arlene.

12. Glendora Cessna, deceased, McKeesport, Pa., married F. W. Schweitzer. Issue: Leslie, Raymond, Howard, Frank, Earl, Richard, Glen, Robert, Harry.

13. Louise Cessna, Latrobe, Pa., married Harry R. Hummer. Issue: Harry C.

14. Lorenzo Dow Cessna, Salem, Ohio, married Margaret Kohout. Issue: Clifford, Kathryn.

Thank you for our nice visit at your home, and we want you and Mrs. Cessna to visit us some time.

Sincerely yours,

Louise C. Hummer,
(Mrs. Harry R.)
621 Spring Street.

The House of Cessna

Evanston, Illinois, June 30, 1935.

Dear Cousin Howard Cessna:

Your very nice letter was not forwarded to me in the country, so I am late in replying.

I do not know the proper form, but here is the information for your records.

John Cessna IV (1768-1813).

Elizabeth (1795-1875) daughter of John; m. Peter Morgart.

Ellen (1821-1904) daughter of Elizabeth; m. Robert Hafer.

Mary Elizabeth (1846-1915) daughter of Ellen; m. Thomas Ough.

Gertrude Margaret, b. 1876, daughter of Mary Elizabeth; m. Mord E. Pangle.

Mary Ellen, b. 1903, daughter of Gertrude Margaret.

I do hope I may get to visit "our family's" territory and have the pleasure of knowing you and your family. I am eager to hear you tell all the interesting stories I know you can.

Thank you very much for your interest.

Very sincerely yours,

Gertrude Ough Pangle.

CHAPTER XIV

History

Coming to America in the Early Days Was Hazardous

From the beginning till about 1776—65000 Germans alone landed at Philadelphia.

Some captains were wicked murders of souls; others were more considered.

Most of the Germans came down the Rhine to Rotterdam—often requiring from May to October, amid such hardship as no one is able to describe. Boats had to pass 26 custom houses; ships examined when it suited so as to make passengers spend money.

At Holland it was the same—often 6 weeks of a delay—and because provisions etc. were dear there, the poor spent nearly all they had. From there to England generally at Cowes the Isle of Wright—some at Deal, Dover or Portsmouth. Amsterdam in Holland was another starting point.

At these places frequently another delay of a couple weeks followed—either to pass custom houses or waiting for favorable wind.

Then the misery began for eight, nine or twelve weeks. The passengers packed like herrings without proper food or water were subject to all diseases such as dysentery, scurry, typhoid and smallpox.

Children died in large numbers—32 on our ship.

One day, relates a passenger, just as we had a heavy gale a woman on our ship who was to give birth, was pushed through the port hole and dropped into the sea because she was far in the rear of the ship and could not be brought forward.

The misery reached the climax when a gale raged for two or three nights and days, causing all to think the ship was going to the bottom. The people would cry and pray most pitiously. In such a gale the sea raged and surged so that waves rose like mountains and often tumbled over the ship. No one could walk, sit or lie and were tumbled over one another—both the sick and the well. Such caused many to die.

Another delay at Province Island where all must be examined before landing. On this Island in 1754, 253 were buried in one year. $30 to $60 was the cost for the trip. A list printed in a paper on hand bill stating how many were to be sold. Those with money were freed.

One cannot appreciate better what each star and stripe in our Flag has cost, than to learn the motive that impelled our ancestors to leave their boyhood homes and acquaintances to hazard such a journey.

The few saying to the many, "you go produce the bread and we'll eat it," religious persecution, and always war, were among some of the causes.

SHARPSHOOTER

Uhrichsville, O.—(AP)—Mrs. Mildred Cessna of Cadiz is not one who does things by halves. She:

Attained a perfect score of 300 as a member of the Uhrichsville rifle club.

Achieved a string of 44 consecutive bull's eyes.

And enabled her club to defeat the Barnesville club in a shootoff, 1494 points to 1477.

THE CONGRESSMAN'S JOKE

Tom Corwin, famous Ohio statesman and popular orator of a century ago, has a keen sense of humor, and because of his dark complexion, played a joke on an obsequious tavern keeper one time that was often related up and down the length of the National road at Washington.

Tom in his early days was a wagoner, a driver of freight wagon trains along the great east-west highway, and the rallying cry of his friends in the campaign that elected him governor of Ohio was, "Hurrah for Tom Corwin, the wagoner boy!"

Because of his dark complexion, Tom frequently was mistaken for a negro by strangers. At that time the race distinction was very much pronounced.

Once, when he was a member of Congress, he passed over the National road in a chartered coach in company with Henry Clay and other distinguished gentlemen, en route to Washington, D. C.

The party stopped one day at an old stage tavern, kept by Samuel Cessna at the foot of Town hill, in a place also known as "Snib Hollow," 5 miles east of Cumberland, Md. Cessna was fond of entertaining guests and was particularly anxious to cater to these distinguished travelers.

The tall form of Tom Corwin attracted his attention. He noted Tom's swarthy complexion and heard his companions call him Tom and supposed he was the servant of the party. Cessna had met Clay before and knew him.

The party ordered dinner and then someone suggested drinks all around to relieve the tedium of travel and excite an appetite for the expected dinner. Cessna hurried to his storeroom and produced a bottle of fine old cognac, the "tony" drink of the old pike. The finest drink of the day was brandy and loaf sugar, lighted by a taper and burnt. Popular tradition had it that "if burnt brandy couldn't save a man" in need of physical relaxation, his case was hopeless.

The zealous old landlord produced the drink, and handed it first to the other gentlemen in Corwin's party. After each of the others had stepped up to the bar and been served, Cessna, in a patronizing way, offered a glass to Corwin, saying:

"Tom, you take a drink."

Corwin drank off the glass in an humble manner and returned it to the landlord with modest thanks. The others in the party saw what was transpiring and kept straight faces.

Dinner then was announced and when the party entered the dining room, they saw that a side table, after the custom of the time, had been set for their "servant."

Corwin went over to the side table and sat down, while the others gathered around the sumptuous feast at the main table.

The House of Cessna

"We have one hundred men working at Fort Morris, with heart and hand, every day." Fort Morris was built on a rocky hill, at the western end of the town. The walls were two feet in thickness.

Among the suffers of this region was one who revenged himself terribly upon the savages. He was a white man, known as Captain Jack, the "Black Hunter," the "Black Rifle," the "Wild Hunter of the Juniata," the "Black Hunter of the Forest," etc. His real name was never ascertained, but his exploits were household topics of conversation.

Following the incursions of July, 1757, others were killed in the autumn of that year near Carlisle, and many victims of similar raids in the years following until the conclusion of the Pontiac war.

In the summer of 1761 many fled for shelter and protection to Shippensburg and Carlisle. In July, 1763, 1,384 of the poor, distressed back inhabitants took refuge in Shippensburg. Of this number 301 were men, 345 women and 738 children. Many of these unfortunate refugees were compelled to lie in barns, cellars and under leaky roofs, as the dwelling houses were crowded.

In the lower end of the county every house, barn and stable was crowded, horses, cattle, harvests and everything which they could not carry in their flight. They were reduced to abject beggary and despair.

The streets and roads were filled with people; the men distracted with grief for their losses; and the desire for revenge more keenly excited by the disconsolate females and bereaved children who wailed around them.

Between Fort Morris and Fort Loudon, the next provincial defense was the stone dwelling house of Benjamin Chambers, surrounded by water from Falling Spring, the present site of Chambersburg.

Fort Loudon was located one mile distant from the present town of Loudon, Franklin county. It was the place where the public stores were safely kept and also served as a barracks for the troops of that vicinity. Fort Littleton, the last defensive work in the chain, was at Sugar Cabins, in the northern end of

Fulton county. During its most stirring history Captain Hance Hamilton was in command of its garrison.

On the other side of Fort Morris the nearest provincial defense was Fort Lowther, in the center of the present borough of Carlisle. It was at the latter fort that Governor Morris was stationed, June 5, 1755, to be near Braddock's army and render such assistance as might be required.

It was at Fort Lowther, in 1764, that more than four hundred unfortunate captives, who had been released from the Indians by Colonel Henry Bouquet, were brought, and where many of them were restored to their overjoyed relatives.

—*Altoona Mirror, July 17, 1927.*

The French in Pennsylvania

It will be 174 years next month since 454 French companions of Evangeline were thrown by the British into Pennsylvania.

These were a group of 7000 ill-fated Acadian exiles. Many of them later became a public charge upon the townships where they dwelt.

But neither these doomed Acadian refugees nor any other large group of French ever clung closely enough together in Pennsylvania to form a real colonial settlement.

Thousands of Huguenots and of Catholic French migrated from their homeland to this State, but they were widely scattered and German and English pioneers often changed the French names.

For this reason the French frontiersmen in Pennsylvania have received less than their due from local historians.

Hence I commend Dr. Wayland F. Dunaway of Pennsylvania State College for his recent effort to resurrect the early Pennsylvania French.

He calls attention to many names to which I have referred in the past—French family names that have been so grossly altered as to cause many a one of French blood to imagine he was of Pennsylvania German or British origin.

The House of Cessna

It is a fact that a greater number of French settled in Pennsylvania than any other colony except South Carolina.

They began to come years before Penn arrived. Jacquet, Haes, Hypolite, Boyer and Grange were Frenchmen who had homes on the Delaware before Penn got out of Oxford.

Long ago, however, the common French prefix "de" and "la" disappeared from scores of family names.

You wouldn't recognize him as Senator Mathew Stanley le Quay, but such was his real name and he was a Frenchman.

General Pershing's first American ancestor was a Pennsylvania Frenchman.

General John F. Reynolds, Lancaster's Civil War hero, killed at Gettysburg, was a Frenchman, too, and direct descendant of famous Madame Ferree.

That lady colonist—one of the few in all America—planted her French settlement in Lancaster.

French flocked along the Schuylkill and the Perkiomen Valleys.

There was Hillegas, who gave a Treasurer to the United States in Michael, whose portrait you have seen thousands of times on paper money.

Boyertown was founded by Beyer, a Frenchman.

Purviance, LeBar, Le Fever, Le Shar, now usually spelled Lesher, Perdeau, changed to Barto; Dubois and Trego, are only a few I could mention.

It is said that 7000 people up Easton way can trace their ancestry to the three Le Bar brothers who settled at the Delaware Water Gap.

I wonder if the French were not ahead of the Germans in old Berks county, which later became so strongly tinged with German customs, thrift, progress and wealth?

Well, there were French in Oley Valley prior to 1710. And there still linger in Berks many notable French names, such as Keim, de Banneville, De Turk, Bartolet, Bertolet, Le Van.

Also Plank, which was originally de La Planch, and which doesn't remind you of the great Southpaw Eddie of Gettysburg.

Naturally Germantown was settled first by Germans, and

yet French dropped down there when that village was an infant.

There was Jean Le Brun. Did he become plain John Brown?

There was James De la Plaine, and I'm sure that was changed into the well known Delaplaine of today.

The Leverings, of course, not only gave us a distinguished bishop and a Prohibition candidate for President of the United States, but Levering Mill road in Cynwyd.

General Atterbury, of course, is proud of his Boudinot ancestor who was an eminent Philadelphia Frenchman.

Nowhere did the French cling together in large enough groups to exert any important political influence.

Welsh did differently, and so you see scores of Welsh place names fastened permanently upon the map of Southeastern Pennsylvania.

On the contrary, the French left few place names and, frequently, as I've said, lost their own.

Two English land speculators, Vincent and Coxe, bought 20,000 acres of land in Chester county and tried to create there a great Huguenot colony.

About the only relic of that venture is seen in the names of East and West Vincent townships.

La Porte is one French name which survives in the county seat of Sullivan county.

When German neighbors insisted upon calling the Frenchman Lapierre, not that but Stein, or English neighbors called him plain Mr. Stone, the Frenchman, being in a decided minority, was helpless.

Had they lived so thickly in one county as to be bosses of local offices and local schools, the French pioneers in Pennsylvania might have put the boot on the other foot. In that case the German Kiefer might have come down to posterity as Tonnelier.

But the Germans, even in those counties where they were always most numerous, were not able to keep English place names off the map.

I heard one distinguished German explain that in this sentence: "Our ancestors did the work while the English ran the offices.—*Girard, in Philadelphia Inquirer, Oct. 5, 1929.*

CHAPTER XV

Autobiography of Howard Cessna

INTERESTING NOTES OF EARLY SETTLERS—HOWARD CESSNA
COMPLIES WITH REQUEST OF HON. OSCAR W. SMITH, FORMER
EDITOR OF INQUIRER.

———

Santa Barbara, Calif., Jan. 29, 1934.

Mr. Howard Cessna,
  Bedford, Pa.

Dear Friend: I read your splendid article on Martin Hill in both Bedford newspapers. I have cut it out and intend to paste it in my history of Bedford County. Accept my congratulations.

There are more historical articles concerning Bedford County that should be rescued from oblivion before they are forgotten. What has been done about the old Friend Graveyard north of Rainsburg? The last time I saw it, in 1926, it was overgrown with weeds and brush and the headstones were barely visible. An article about the "Friends" would be timely. With kind regards, I am,

Very sincerely yours,
Oscar W. Smith.

Bedford, Pa., Feb 13, 1934.

Dear Friend: Since you live so far away from your boyhood grees below, and such weather makes us all envy you in Cali- As I write this, the thermometer is hovering around fourteen degrees below, and such weather makes us all envy you in California with summer weather the year around. However, I am consoled by remembering what the late Judge Hall said: His ancestor, our first U. S. Senator Wm. McClay, wrote to a prospective colony of emigrants: "Come to Pennsylvania—it's between the two great extremes, hot and cold, free from floods, draughts, and earthquakes." (Reader, this is in the nature of a whisper so Oscar can't hear it. Our former Friend's Cove boy has made good in the West. His neighbors sent him to the State Legislature and later he became State President of an Insurance Company).

"Father Time" is leading both of us nearer the sunset, and if we can add a little local history before too late, I presume its our duty. Someone has said "in the death of most every aged citizen (you and I are not old yet) some local history is lost. Had you and myself, when we were young lads, interviewed men like Samuel Williams or even his son, George, or William Smith, and made note of their facts stated, we could have preserved so much more than now obtainable.

Just recently Mrs. Helen Shaffer Hill examined these graves and her report corresponds with your descriptions. I obtained a copy of what she found legible. The record follows: Jh. Friend, Father, Ye 22-1778, age 76. Joseph Friend, Apr. 28-1806, age 89. Jas. Patterson or Potterion, 64 yrs. 1700.

From the dates on these tombstones, you will observe John Friend was too old to have taken part in the Revolutionary War, but would be of the right age to have taken part in the French and Indian War and, as they lived in Virginia, then to there we must go for their record.

In those early days parents were more strict than now. John Friend in his will showed his disapproval of his son's actions in these words: "But if it please God that Joseph, my son, should quit all his evil practices and truly and sincerely reform and take to industry, he shall have his share in my estate." Evidently his son made good, as later in his will he gave or sold his slave "Dick," then in Kentucky, as well as large tracts of land in Kentucky. This father willed around 3,000 acres in Tennessee. His daughter Elizabeth married a Mr. Taylor.

In Pennsylvania archives we learn John Friend, Philip Friend and Tobias Friend served in Revolutioary War, west of the Alleghenies. These soldiers in all probability were grandsons of either John or Joseph Friend. As I write this, on my desk is a patent to Joseph Friend for 132 acres and 48 perches surveyed in 1762 calling for adjoiners, as follows: Wm. McClay (first U. S. Senator of Penna.) now owned by Thos. Cessna, Pendergrass (second settler at Bedford, who had three log houses burned while there, and a daughter killed and scalped by the Indians) and Ecart Worley. On a guess I'd say this tract was the Rose farm now owned by John Cessna, Jr. At least, its my first information as to where Pendergrass settled and the exact farm can be learned.

Joseph Friend had more land than this. John had what we now know as the Elwood Williams farm and Joseph the Carl Fisher land. But enough about land—let us look at the frontier picture as it must have been seen by them—the Friends.

The Ohio Company claimed 400,000 acres west of the Allegheny Mountains. They sent a surveyor by the name of Christopher Gist to examine the land they claimed and make a report. He was a surveyor, a native of North Carolina. Gist set out on his journey from Old Town, Maryland, Wednesday, Oct. 31, 1750. He followed the old Indian path along Warrior Ridge, north 30 degrees east, a distance of 21 miles in Southampton Township (of course, there was no township then). The next day they journey due north one mile and north 30 degrees east three miles. There Gist took sick and they remained all night. On Saturday they proceeded north eight miles to the Juniata River, where they stayed all night.

From the above, it will be seen an Indian trail either came through Chaneysville Gap or Sweet Root Gap, as it would be impossible to go due north in Black Valley. Our mountains run north 30 degrees east and in Friend's Cove he could go due north. This was the first white man in Friend's Cove who left a record. Before him over the same trail might have gone Thos. Kinton, David Priest, John Walker, George Crogan, John Frazer, John Harris, Robert Ray, Dunning or Ferguson—all Indian traders, guided by friendly Indians. Quoting from Judge Hall, these "early traders and frontier settlers must have had nerve of steel and eyes like eagles." These men came here about 1762.

It was six years later when citizens at Bedford petitioned officials down east for land on which to build a union church, saying there was no church within seventy miles. Pack horses, with wooden frames on their back and each horse tied to the tail of one in front, was the mode of transportation. It is said some of the first settlers to have any grist ground had to go as far as Chambersburg or Hagerstown, Md. Their radio was three shots fired in succession, which meant they should do the same to warn others farther away to hurry to the Fort or Block House, the Indians were coming. Their telephone was a slight peck after night on the window (sometimes made of greased paper) which meant "don't kindle the fire but hurry to the block house." Their food was such that if it were possible for one of them to return and walk into a modern grocery store, they could not believe their own eyes—much less the merchant's explanation. But my, what men and what rifle shots were they!

The children of John and Joseph Friend left Friend's Cove and pushed on further into the frontier. It's only proper that I quote from W. H. Welfley's account of two sons—Capt. Andrew Friend and his brother Augustine:

"Capt. Andrew Friend, one of the early pioneers who settled in the Turkeyfoot region, was a noted hunter and Indian fighter. According to best accounts that we have of him, his ancestors had settled in the valley of Virginia (Shenandoah) where they owned large estates. They were of English origin. Over the water the family had been of some note, and among them were some who had been prominent both in state and church. In the civil wars they had adhered to the fortunes of the house of Stuart and, finding themselves on the losing side, some of the family emigrated to Virginia, settling in the Shenandoah Valley, where Andrew Friend is supposed to have been born. The family, at one time wealthy, because somewhat reduced in circumstances, left Virginia, going into Eastern Pennsylvania. But John and Joseph Friend, two brothers, went westward and settled in Colerain Township, Cumberland (now Bedford) County, in

The House of Cessna

a beautiful and fertile valley that is encompassed by mountains on three sides and is to this day known as Friend's Cove.

"Andrew Friend and his brother Augustine are supposed to have been sons of one of these two brothers. While yet young men, Andrew and his brother, being of an adventurous turn and at the same time enthusiastic hunters, hearing of these mountains full of all kinds of game, went to the mouth of Wills Creek, or Fort Cumberland, which was then considered one of the most advanced of the frontier settlements. From there, frequent excursions were made into the mountainous regions to the westward. This, of course, was in a region forbidden to white men, and those who entered it did so at their own peril."

Augustine Friend settled in what is now Garrett County, Maryland, and his descendants are looked upon today as among the best citizens. Tradition has it that Andrew Friend was with Washington on his western journey, was with the Braddock Expedition and served in the French War. He was frequently placed in command of local companies organized for defense against the Indians. He particularly hated the Deleware and Shawnee tribes and with his unerring rifle sent more than one of them to the happy hunting ground, although it is said he never killed an Indian woman or child, only in self-defense. On one occasion after a settler's house had been burned, Friend, being called to the place, saw in the woods nearby an Indian carring a looking glass on his back and it was the sun on the glass that attracted his attention. Raising his rifle he fired at the glass, putting a hole through both it and the Indian. On several occasions afterwards Friend expressed regret that he had shot him on circumstantial evidence.

In a recent article I mentioned the fact that Negro Mt. was named in honor of a giant slave of Friend who had been killed in the battle with the Indians. Quoting further from Mr. Welfley's article, "The Indians had learned to know and fear Friend and made several attempts to capture him. On one occasion while hunting, he had just shot a wild turkey. Two Indians suddenly sprang at him from a cover. They had guns and could perhaps have shot him, but as his gun was then empty, they thought they might capture him alive; had they succeeded it is easy to see what his fate would have been. Friend was a swift runner and started off at his best speed, with the Indians close behind him. For a while he held his lead, but one of his moccasins becoming untied, he began to lose ground and the Indians gained on him. They were headed towards a precipice. Friend knew this but kept on at his best speed. The Indians were quite near and sure of their man but with a mighty jump he cleared the trunk of a tree and found himself at the bottom of the precipice with only a few bruises. On one occasion, with a neighbor, they discovered a herd of eight or ten buffalo; one of these —a fine, fat, young bull—they shot, the rest escaped. It is said this was the last buffalo killed and the last herd seen in that section.

Captain Friend was popular among those who knew him, a genial, kind-hearted and generous man, never quarrelsome or contentious, without any frills or fringes except on his buckskin hunting shirt. He was also a man of fair education for those days. He was rather tall and slim in figure, very strong, active and wiry and of unusual agility. Even in his old age he was straight as an arrow and always carried himself erect.

Somewhere bout 1775 Jonathan Cessna, who was married to Mary Friend of Friend's Cove, Bedford County, Pa., emigrated from there to Kentucky, where Louisville now stands on the banks of the Ohio River, cleared two acres of land, the first cleared within the limits of the metropolis. Soon after he was killed by the Indians, leaving his son, William, aged three years, who remembered the last time he saw his father by the following incident: The whites having made preparations to go out on an Indian raid, had collected on the banks of the Ohio River, at what is now Louisville, to execute their intention. Jonathan took his son, William, in his arms, kissed him goodbye, and told him to be a good boy and obey his mother. He never returned to his pleasant cabin home or his beloved family, but was numbered with the slain.

Mary Friend, above mentioned, was a daughter of either John or Joseph Friend, of whom we write, and her son was able

[Handwritten annotations in margins and across top:]

Jonathan Cessna was Killed in 1793 when his son was 3 yrs old So in 1809 when Lincoln was born He — William was 19 yrs of age only so he could not have been a judge at that age so this Judge William must have been an older William Cessna probably the one who came west with Gen. Muhlenberg

142   The House of Cessna

to extend the first act of kindness later in life to Abraham Lincoln, which fact alone should make it necessary on the part of any patriot to preserve those graves.

The following is copied from McClure's Magazine of Nov. 1895, Vol. 5, No. 6:

"At the time of Abraham Lincoln's birth his father was away from home. Some of Mrs. Lincoln's neighbors, who were with her at the event, learned that she was destitute of anything in the nature of food. Some of the ladies called upon Judge William Cessna, one of the most prominent men of that time in this section, in Mrs. Lincoln's behalf, and he donated flour and other articles of food." —Howard Cessna.

SOME BEDFORD COUNTY HISTORY

AN ADDRESS DELIVERED JULY 14, 1934, BEFORE THE WESTERN HISTORICAL SOCIETY AT BEDFORD, PA., BY HOWARD CESSNA, ESQ., A MEMBER OF THE BEDFORD COUNTY BAR.

Honored Guests: I wish to compliment your Society on the object of your tour and to remind you that some philosopher of life has said "He who knows no history is but a child."

From cellars and attics have been brought historical heirlooms and placed in show windows for you and the public to observe, on account of your coming, which, together with others, ought to be placed for all time in some building here.

If I were to go on the air as radio announcer for Bedford, I'd imitate Atlanta, Georgia, "down where the South begins," only I'd change it and say "This is Bedford, where the U. S. began."

Thomas Montgomery, author of the history of the Forts of Pennsylvania says: There would be no U. S. Flag, no U. S. Constitution and no U. S. Government, had it not been for sacrifice and patriotism of the Frontier Citizens.

Take out of the U. S. History, first, the driving of the

French of America, then the English and forcing the Indians back—and the rest of our history is common place indeed.

Here is where the troops rendezvous—7000 of them; the American Troops coming from the North, East, and South to join The King's Highlanders—men in Kilts.

But permit me to digress a little so as to give you some of our local history. We have no battle fields to show you, yet two military engagements took place in the real early days, that clearly show our ancestors were not only loyal friends in May but in December as well.

Some merchants down East, desiring to establish trade with the Indians West of the Allegheny, loaded up a pack horse train of about 80 horses—Each horse tied to the tail of the one in front, with a wooden frame on the horse. On the horses were found scalping knives, tomahawks, guns, powder and shot. Twice they were notified to turn and go back East as the Indians were killing too many and it was dangerous to take such implements of death among them. The merchants only laughed at them.

James Smith selected men whom he could trust and they cut through the forest to the little stream running through Everett. There he had his men to blacken and two to a tree with orders not to shoot any thing but a horse and no one to shoot until his partner had loaded his rifle. It didn't take long until the merchants cried out, "What would you have us do?" Pile all your goods at one end of the trail and head back East and be quick about it. Everett was called Bloody Run for a century afterwards.

This same Smith learning some of his followers were placed in irons in Fort Bedford, sent word to the Captain of the Fort he was coming to get his friends out of prison. Again he selected those in whom he had faith and set off to capture Fort Bedford. He had, as a spy, William Thompson, who later became a General in Revolutionary War. When Smith got to the Juniata Crossings, he went into camp so as to fool the Captain of the Fort, but that night, at 11:00 o'clock, he got his men up and quietly marched to near the Fort to await report from

The House of Cessna

Thompson. About daylight Thompson slipping along the river bank, to about where Lysinger's Mill is, told Smith now was the time. The gate to the North was open, the men had gone for a dram and breakfast, that he'd run ahead and in the Fort he'd run to where the guns were stacked, so they'd know how to keep the guards from repossessing them. This was speedily done, the prisoners taken to a blacksmith shop and the irons filed off. This was the first Fort captured in America from the British.

In both of these military engagements no life was lost.

This James Smith must have been the Bill Cody of his day, here in the Frontier.

A little to the North of the Crossings is a monument to Mr. White—a member of the Boston Tea Party. He was a blacksmith by trade and England would not allow the Colonies to even make their own nails. Not only tea, but everything had a tax and nothing was allowed to be shipped to this Country without a tax—save a negro—a slave.

A little West of this monument was Fort Piper—a haven of safety for thousands in the frontier day. It's site is not marked.

At the Crossings is an old wooden bridge, over a hundred years old. Through it went the early immigrants in Conestoga Wagons, frequently drawn by five yolk of oxen or The Concord Coach, drawn by six mules.

These immigrants now are the ancestors of our present western Governors, Senators and Congressmen. Many went through that bridge, probably singing Susannah or Annie Laurie, only to fill an unknown grave along the trail of the great West.

Through it went many a drove of sheep, cattle, hogs or turkeys to market. On a dusty day people frequently had to get in the forest off the road to avoid the dust. Most all the stone houses now standing were Taverns that furnished a market for the farmers better than exists today.

Just below this bridge are the abutments of still an older bridge—a chain bridge—That carried over earlier settlers and the French and Indian Troops. It was the first bridge across the Juniata.

On this side of Everett was the Indian Village of Queen Allaquippa to whom Washington gave a shawl and bottle of whiskey. In his diary he wrote, she seemed to appreciate the bottle more than the shawl. The site is also unmarked, as well as The Indian Village near Schellsburg, known as the Shawnee Village.

The top of Wills Mountain was the underground railroad that guided scores and scores of slaves to Fishertown among the friendly Quakers, who rushed them on North to Canada.

When Seth Parker was giving, over the Air—secrets of the sea—he showed a Village in England where drowned seamen only, were placed in a vault and in opening this vault—not once but often—to place therein other coffins, to their amazement, the coffins would be standing on end. So, we have the mystery of the Mountain or rather a Dream. In the Northern end of the county, we have a monument to the Lost Cox Children, who were lost in 1856. Thousands quit work to go help search. A Mr. Dibert, who lived some fifteen miles away and had never been in the Blue Knob Mountain, dreamed three nights in succession, that he was searching for these children. Each trip, in his dream, was the same. Telling his wife of this, she urged him to go to his brother-in-law, who knew the Mountain and see if he could find the route his dream took him. This he did and when he saw the Mountain, as in his dream, he said down there we'll find a dead deer, farther on, one little shoe and then we cross a run, now known as Bobbs Creek, and after turning up a hollow we'll find the two dead children.

If our Majestic Mountain could speak they could give us thrill after thrill of frontier occurances. They could ask how you, of Pittsburgh, would return, had you come here 200 years ago? No doubt they saw the buffalo make the first path centuries ago across the Allegheny Mountain and later used by the Indians as the Kittanning Trail, over which went the prisoners and scalps taken by the Indians. It was not until 1749 Col. Chesup got an Indian, by the name of Nemacola, to lay out another Trail, now The National Pike. No doubt these Mountains saw the smoke rise in the Big Cove when the Indians killed 50 families in one day. When their neighbors came later, they saw horses, with three to five arrows shot into them, standing

The House of Cessna

slowly dying by the ashes of their owners home. Perhaps they would tell us of 600 prisoners brought back at one time and some had been in captivity so long that indentification was difficult. One mother sang in German, an old hymn to attract her daughter, who was taken when quite young. They would tell us that nowhere from New York to Georgia, was greater zeal for the Revolutionary War shown against Tories and those who refused to go to War, than here around Bedford.

Yes, when word came from Concord and Lexington, from the frontier here went real fighters to Boston—700 miles—and took the lead for having the best guns and best marksmen. When they went through New York, they gave an exhibition which consisted of shooting while the regiment was on the run, at a target seven inches square, at a distance of two hundred yards. They saw service from Canada to Georgia. The red blood of courage shown by those frontier citizens has not turned to water in the fourth and fifth generation. It has been shown in our later wars, and has kept our Flag from trailing in the dust.

In the face of so glorious a past, it's puzzling to read of preachers agreeing not to support war; of students refusing to stand when our National Song is sung.

When I run across such—I think of our glorified dead and especially do I think "If you break faith with us, we shall not sleep, though poppies grow in Flander's Field."

When we think of the Infinite Being able to arrange the Universe so we fall 1008 miles per minute; of His emptying the horn of plenty on the U. S. so that we possessed two-thirds of the world's wealth, seven-tenth of all the automobiles, telephones, radios, and produced two men who have left greater amounts to charity and for research work to aid the human family, than all the Kings and wealth of past ages—I am convinced that this generation and those to follow will not break faith with those who made the supreme sacrifice by giving their lives that we might carry on.

This Depression has been awful. That red blood of courage, handed down to us, has shown its quality through these trying times.

Bancroft, who spent 26 years preparing his History, tells us, God's presence is not seen where the battle is going on, but when the smoke clears away, lo, there stands God.

Let us hope when the Depression is over, we will see benefits follow, such as Lincoln complained of existing in ages gone by "A few saying to the many, you work and produce the bread and we'll eat it."

Our constitution, if necessary, may be amended to cover all remedies necessary.

I believe our country will continue to move upward to that condition of which statesmen have dreamed and poets have sung.

—Howard Cessna, Esq.

MARTIN HILL

HOW THE LARGE STATE GAME PRESERVE IN THIS COUNTY WAS OBTAINED—REMINISCENCES OF EARLIER DAYS.

Recently an official in the Forestry Department asked me to write the History of Martin Hill in so far as my relation to it in a business sense was concerned.

At first I dismissed the idea as of no interest to the public at present or the future. Later, I began to compare its history to oncoming generations with that of the real early history of Friend's Cove, which has caused me to wish scores of times that those early settlers had kept a dairy similar to Christopher Gist, who was the first white man to come into the Cove, 1739, and leave a record of the event in his diary.

Just why did the first three settlers at Bedford, viz: Ray, Pendergrass and Fredrigal, after being run off and houses burned by the Indians at Bedford, come and settle in Friend's Cove? What protection had the Friends and Cessnas, who apparently were unmolested by the Indians; did they have a block-house or Fort here, else did they have protection from some friendly Indians? The generation that could have answered these questions have passed on and all such information has passed over the horizon into oblivion.

The House of Cessna

To avoid any similar neglect to future generations as to the history of Martin Hill, I am prompted to pen my connection with the State purchase of it. Should it grow in importance in the next 100 years as it has in the past 25, its early history will be of interest.

THE NAMING OF MARTIN HILL—Often I've wondered at the name and just as often dropped my guess by coming to the conclusion that possibly it was named in honor of James Martin, one of the Revolutionary patriots who, with men like Daugherty and Col. Armstrong, conducted our court before our constitution; again I'd imagine it was named in Maryland after some frontier character.

At least its name is not as easily traced as that of its neighbor, the Wills Mountain. Judge Hall tells us it was named in honor of an Indian Chief—a man of large size, who was buried in a sitting posture on Wills Mountain, above Bedford, about 100 years ago. Some physician from Baltimore violated the grave and carried away the bones, which were very large.

Nor is its name as easily traced as Negro Mountain in Somerset County, Pa. That was named in honor of a giant slave who accompanied Augustus Friend in pursuit of Indians who had killed and scalped frontier settlers. In the battle 18 out of 19 Indians were killed after the white men discovered their neighbor, whom the Indians had taken as prisoner, hanging on a tree, skinned, perhaps alive.

In the battle the negro slave was mortally wounded and the white men, anxious to return to their families were about to desert the slave but Augustus Friend, who was cradled at the foot of Martin Hill, said no, he'd not leave him; that his blood, though that of a black man, had been shown to be loyal and that he'd remain behind with him. When he died Friend took a hollow log and buried him and the mountain has ever since been called Negro Mountain.

Martin Mountain, like the Wills Mountain, ends abruptly. The Dan Blankley Knob is its northern end, connected by "cow bone hollow" and the Wertz Knob to Evitts Mountain. So Martin Hill must have been named from the mountain of which it is a part, the main mountain extending to the south.

MY FIRST INTEREST IN MARTIN HILL—In the summer of 1896 I discovered, one afternoon in my office in Everett, a Court decision that would permit unseated land sold for taxes under certain conditions to be redeemed. This ruling of the court was just the opposite of what my old friends at the Bedford Bar had advised me. I recall vividly the hot weather on that particular afternoon and the joy I felt at discovering an opportunity to gradually work myself into owning many acres of land—notwithstanding many regarded the whole mountain worthless.

I recall hearing a mountaineer about that time say, in a spirit of boasting, that he had often set the mountain afire in order to get through the brush easily. Another citizen, regarded as having good judgment, met me coming out of the mountain and greeted me by saying "Howard, have you lost your wits? Don't you know your father and Dan Cessna broke up monkeying with Martin Hill and you will end the same?" On coming home from Everett, I mean going to Rainsburg where my parents lived, late one night I heard my father and brother talking in the dark, not knowing I was so near. Father said, "Howard must be going crazy to fool so much time over Martin Hill."

Therefore, the State Reservation, as now improved by good roads, camp sites, etc., has been made possible by the discovery of that court decision. Had I not begun adding to the original tracts so obtained, no big body of land could have been offered to induce the State to purchase. "From little acorns giant white oaks grow." I must have met discouraging remarks in keeping with Cato's thought 2,000 years ago: go contrary to custom and you'll always be right.

In the early days of our Commonwealth, in Philadelphia especially, there existed characters with a hunch to lay warrants and secure large bodies of land. Land was cheap. Someone has said that Wm. Penn was a top-notcher when dealing in real estate for he secured Pennsylvania, for around $2.50 per square mile and then sold it for 25c per acre. At any rate, these individuals would use other people's names, generally those living in the neighborhood, and the warrants were mostly for 400 acres.

The House of Cessna

Evidently, some one became involved financially. The Bank of North America or its representative had to take over the tracts and, becoming dissatisfied at paying tax, sold and allowed to be sold their holdings.

My uncle, John Cessna, and later G. W. and Dan Cessna, tanners at Rainsburg, obtained title. When the firm of the latter went out of business, they secured my brother's indebtedness against them by giving a judgment note, upon which an execution was issued that passed their title to their mountain land as well as their tannery. Using these tracts as a nucleus, I bought adjoining tracts from individuals and at Treasurer's Sale until in all I sold around 16,000 acres. In fact, from my present farm south to the Mason and Dixon Line, I sold to the State. This was not all in one sale. I had some tracts at first sale with title not perfected and it took several years to finish my sales with the State. I'll not give details of sales as court record show.

EXPERIENCES—Varied indeed were some of my efforts to obtain adjoining tracts to connect up my holdings. Right in the heart of my main body of land was what an old-timer would call a squatter. Oscar Doty and I gave him 300 sheep to look after. Many of the lambs disappeared, with scores of old ones. We tried our plan but once. Many years after this party, in conversation with a very distant relative of mine said he "ate so much mutton that year that he could taste wool yet."

In that fellow's day on Martin Hill deer season was all the time and many a mountain fire took the place of what we now call "men on the drive." But even before this, somewhere in the early 80's a heavy sleet or crust on the deep snow made it possible for Adam Garlick to slaughter the deer. He borrowed my red sleigh—the first bit of personal property I ever owned—to haul off Martin Hill the hindquarters of 22 deer. The sleigh broke down near the "crooked pine crossing" and years and years afterwards I saw the irons of it by the roadside. In those days it was not uncommon for hunters to have deer licks and a stone blind erected within gunshot of the lick, or a platform on a tree near by. It seems incredible, but occasionally at these licks a wire, running down from the lick to the trigger of a cocked shot gun, could be seen.

With the aid of a surveyor—generally Lewis Pittman—I surveyed practically all the tracts sold to the State. I recall one occasion when we lived in a tent for two weeks quite near the Dan Blankley spring. The year following some one killed a rattler just where my cot had been located.

In those days it was customary to pasture several hundred head of cattle on Martin Hill, every person who cared to. When night came on, I recall hearing a bull coming out along the foot of Blankley Knob, making the woods echo with his bellowing.

I also recall an incident which perhaps I ought to omit, but there was no noise connected with it. Mr. Pittman and I left Everett on the night of July 4th, after the celebration, and, in keeping with the style of hypocrites, we took a jug of liquor along to help in case of supposed snake-bite. We were traveling in a spring wagon that contained our tent, provisions, etc., and went through Rainsburg just at day break.

When we got our tent up I went for kindling a couple rods away in order to have breakfast soon. When I came back I suggested to Pittman that he get the jug which he had hid in the fern about 10 feet from the spring. He reported that it had been stolen. Both of us felt certain no one was within miles of us that morning but I later imagined a certain fellow in Rainsburg had followed our wagon all the way into Martin Hill just to relieve us of our snake-bite cure.

The first Sunday we were tenting my mother and her niece drove up to pay us a visit. Shortly after their arrival I noticed Pittman carrying on a whispered conversation with my mother. Asking what was wrong mother, laughing until tears were in her eyes, said: "Howard, Mr. Pittman tells me you won't allow him to use soap with which to wash his dishes." I said "Mother don't you recall that Aaron Perdew's bark-peelers—some 80 men—all took sick when a cake of soap fell in the kettle of beans?" From the above you'll observe my knowledge of keeping house.

I was young then and the day's tramp was never too long.

The House of Cessna

Twice Pittman gave out and I took the compass and carried it back to the tent. On each occasion a queer thing happened. The first was down in Wild Cat Hollow on the Bean's Cove side and as he laid down the compass for me to take he picked up a pair of nice large buck horns. The other time we were in Mock's Hollow, upper end of Friend's Cove, and he picked up the largest cow bell I ever saw.

Always I found myself in a rush when the Abstract Title Attorneys were coming to examine my titles. I recall riding in deep snow from Rainsburg to Mr. Somerlot's in Bean's Cove and had my brother's bang-tail saddle horse. To get back to Bedford after getting the papers signed, I left Bean's Cove after dark and cut through Martin Hill instead of following the road over to Chaneysville and around. It was a moon-lit night and as I followed old bark roads to the top of Martin Hill near the present towers—the stillness of the night, the shadows along the hollows and the bright moonlight enchanted me, so I sat on the horse on top of the mountain for quite awhile enjoying the sight and the loneliness.

On another occasion in the previous summer I did not sit on my horse, I was riding a big-boned mule, going to perfect title down on the eastern side of the Tussey, when suddenly a pheasant, with outspread wings, and making its peculiar noise, came out of the brush right at the mule. For a moment I was Bill Rogers, the next moment I wasn't. I landed flat on my back and my derby went over the bank down to a little brooklet. I must have been up rather high to give it such a start.

DR. ROTHROCK—Here was a man! Not large physically but one like the poet admired: "A tall man who lived above the clouds in public acts and private thinking." When he came to examine Martin Hill, I naturally tried to put forth my best foot and efforts. I seem to be one of those characters who when I want to show off I always make a break and sure enough! My first day over the mountain with him on horseback was no exception to the rule. Even after he went home, I made a break. I offered to pick the best apples up at the Zack Wertz place and send him. To this he gave me quite a reprimand saying under no circumstances should I send him the apples—he was in public position and others might interpret it as a bribe. Pennsylvania has not always had men of that calibre.

Well, we started out to inspect Martin Hill. I saw a ground hog on the side of a tree and got off to kill it. He gave a command to get back on, that I should never wantonly kill anything except a snake. I had not gone far until I dismounted again. This time I saw a large black snake. "Get back on, don't kill a black snake;" and along with this command came a talk on snakes. Before the day was over, I thought I had him in shape, for sure. I saw a rattler. Immediately I sprang from my horse and grabbed a small stone. "That's no way to kill a snake," says he. "Take a large stone, hold it over your head and then drop it; you're sure of your mark. The other way, you're apt to miss."

However, in the end he seemed pleased and satisfied, especially admiring my youngest brother Walter and the horse we had given him to ride. Indeed, I'd be ungrateful if I did not more than praise Dr. Rothrock. After my deal with the Department, when he was under no obligation to do what he did, something occurred that showed him to be a real man. A party down east brought suit against me at Bedford, claiming he had used his influence and brought about my sale. When Dr. Rothrock learned of this he sent to the trial Attorney Williams of the Department, who was willing to testify that the plaintiff, on account of past similar actions, was not allowed in their office and had nothing whatever to do with the sale. Of course, the suit was non-suited. If all the departments at Harrisburg were conducted as Dr. Rothrock's was, no scandal would ever be traced there.

EARLY SETTLERS—To go over Martin Hill at present and note the growth of timber on old fields, one is apt to think it impossible that families once lived there and were able to exist. Yet they did. Mr. Bollman, who was recently killed in Snake Spring Township by an automobile, was born there. Dan Blankley, Zack Wertz and Peg Wertz, as well as a Mr. Hutson, had clearings and were able to make a living. Their children came

The House of Cessna

down into Friend's Cove to school in a little log building near Wm. Valentine's. Just below this school house was the Bretz Mill, later owned by my grandfather, Wm. Cessna.

A story is told of Dan Blankley which shows the mountaineer's wit and desire for justice. It seems he was buying wheat from a Friend's Cove farmer and when they were measuring the wheat the farmer said, "Mr. Blankley, I make it a rule never to *stroke* my half-bushel when selling to a neighbor." To this Blankley replied, "If that's the rule, I don't see why you should not *fill* the half bushel."

Just a little distance from the Blankley fields is what used to be called the "Shorty Patch." There is where Joe Ressler, whom I knew for years, built a log house when he was married and went to housekeeping. Later he tore it down, hauled the logs to the top of Ressler Hollow, slid them down the mountain, and used them in a building on his farm.

I've heard old folk tell of quilting bees in those early homes. On one occasion, coming home late, a panther followed and frightened the women. Years ago I talked to the Mr. Perdew, who claimed to have killed the last timber wolf in Big Bear Gap. He also stated his father or grandfather had shoats taken from a log pen by bears coming down from there.

On top of the Smith Knob southwest of Rainsburg, an Indian—likely a chief—was buried and before the Civil War students from Rainsburg Academy dug open the grave.

If those majestic mountains could talk they could reveal historical incidents that would cause our blood to glow and our eyes to sparkle.

I have refused 20 requests to one accepted to make speeches but let me add that no Kinton, Piper or Armstrong can ask me at any reunion and expect a refusal. They were the leaders in the Frontier life that makes it possible to enjoy our automobiles, electricity, refrigerators, etc.

Too often in our civic duties we shut our eyes to those past sacrifices. It will not injure our body politic to hold fast to these thoughts when we cast our votes for men seeking office instead of the newcomers who frequently have not the back-

ground in their ideas of America and for what it stands as do
they.   —Attorney Howard Cessna.

D. A. R. CELEBRATE WASHINGTON'S BIRTHDAY
WITH DINNER

Last Saturday evening the Daughters of the American Revolution dined at the Hotel Washington in honor of Washington's Birthday. Mrs. John Dull, Vice Regent presided in place
of Mrs. Alvin Little, Regent, who was ill. Interesting addresses
were made by Prof. L. H. Hinkle who spoke of Abraham Lincoln, Dr. Americus Enfield who discoursed on the Sons of the
American Revolution and Attorney Howard Cessna, whose address follows:

Madam Regent, Ladies and Gents: Abraham Lincoln said
"The mightiest name on earth is George Washington."

Being one of the wealthiest men of his day, living in absolute
contentment, and knowing if he led America's cause ad failed,
he'd decorate the end of a rope at the hands of the British—we
can see how love for freedom and posterity dominated his soul.

Had he been for self and not for others, our Nation would
not today be the strongest in every particular on earth. Religious and civil liberty might be as a dream yet to come; without
public education the inventive mind of America would never
have produced the hundreds of conveniences that you and I enjoy today, which makes it possible for the humblest to enjoy life
beyond the wildest thoughts of ancient Kings. In fact our
country in the mountainous sections might be like the jungles
of South America and where now exists nearly 100 per cent in-
telligence, 94 per cent illiteracy as found elsewhere may have
followed.

By his ability to inspire confidence in the darkest hours and
his leadership—he led on to a victory that has caused Kings and
Emperors to be dethroned the world around. Yes: had it not
been for Washington no song like "The Yanks Are Coming
Over There" and the Poppies in Flanders would not have been so

patriotically advertised. Democracy would have disappeared from the earth.

With the magic of the radio, almost weekly, we are told by astronomers—the horoscope of men regulate their achievements. They tell us Abraham Lincoln, Chas. Lindberg, Thos. Edison, Longfellow and Washington were all born in the month of February.

While the date of birth is true I am inclined to go back of the Planets to the great creator of all—God. And if you trace Washington's life a kind providential protection seemed to surround him from the beginning. When but a young man near Pittsburgh he was thrown into the river in which cakes of ice were floating, required to spend the night on the Island without fire in frozen clothes; in the morning ice had formed on the water permitting his escape: before reaching Fort Cumberland a supposed friendly Indian shot at him at close range but missed; two horses shot from under him and four bullet holes in his clothing when he collected frontier soldiers and saved the English under Braddock from being annihilated.

Later at Boston a heavy storm permitted the Americans to throw up entrenchments and prevented the British from landing troops from their ship—causing them to retreat. Even in Long Island where the enemy thought they had his army trapped, a heavy fog permitted Washington to escape, and so on to the end.

A lighter heart certainly would have been discouraged from the actions of many of the aristocratic Americans living in the towns and cities becoming Tories—aiding and entertaining the enemy. No wonder he leaned heavily for support from the frontier soldiers who knew not only how to shoot but how to rely on themselves in every emergency.

When Cornwallis surrendered Washington told his men not to cheer and embarrass more the enemy as they marched by to lay down their arms. Posterity will cheer us and that will be sufficient reward. Therefore its more than fitting on this birthday that we hold such gathering and acknowledge the great debt of gratitude we owe him.

And while we acknowledge debts let us not forget to drop a word praising the attitude of organized labor throughout our land.

With millions unemployed, thousands depending on soup-houses, drought stricken districts depending on charity, bank failures by the hundreds—Russia's arch enemy in this country is labor. Not so in many sections of the world. Let us ever be on guard to perpetuate the Democracy which we inherited from Washington and our forefathers.

Let us be like the French bugler Rowland, when the battle was going against the French. Rowland was captured and at the point of the bayonets and cocked rifles was told by his captors to sound the French retreat so as to deceive his countrymen. Without a moments hesitation he sounded the French charge and the on-coming charge ended in victory for France.

—Bedford Gazette, Feb. 27, 1931.

BEDFORD ROTARY CLUB HEARS HISTORICAL SPEAKER.

Bedford Rotary Club met last Tuesday evening at the Hotel Washington and after an excellent repast the members were entertained by Howard Cessna, Esq.

Mr. Cessna, who just recently has been honored by the Institute of American Genealogy of Chicago for his work as a historian of Bedford County spoke to his audience on Bedford's forefathers. He related the trials and tribulations of the pioneer settlers of Fort Bedford, their struggles against the Indians, how the English soldiers camped in this vicinity, the visits of George Washington and of the deeds of James Smith and Charles Gist. He spoke of the fortifications in Bedford, Snake Spring and Everett which was known as Bloody Run. Mr. Cessna summed up his remarks by stating that the courage of our forefathers made possible the more sheltered existence we enjoy today and that this self same courage stood us in good stead during the World War and during the present depression. Relics of pioneer days were also exhibited by Mr. Cessna. At the conclu-

The House of Cessna

sion of his address, Mr. Cessna was unanimously elected an honorary member of Bedford Rotary.

—*Bedford Gazette, April, 1932.*

D. A. R. MEMBERS CELEBRATE FLAG DAY.

More than forty members and guests of the Bedford Chapter, Daughters of American Revolution, enjoyed the gracious hospitality of Atty. and Mrs. Howard Cessna at their country home near Rainsburg on June 14, Flag Day, and celebrated the 155th anniversary of the American Flag.

The century-old stone house was beautifully decorated with flags in keeping with the occasion and the priceless colonial furniture, numerous old deeds, pictures, china, books, etc., with which the house is furnished, proved very interesting and fascinating to every one. A huge flag, covering the entire end of the house, was displayed and had been made by Mrs. Americus Enfield in 1880, when there were but thirty-eight states in the Union.

A delicious cafeteria luncheon was enjoyed, more so because the house was thrown open and one could take a tray and delightfully relax on the lawns, porches or by the huge fireplace to partake of its contents. The hospitality and generosity of the host and hostess were greatly appreciated and the entire day one that long will be pleasantly remembered.

—*Bedford Inquirer, June 17, 1932.*

BEDFORD HISTORIAN ENTERTAINS KIWANIS—TELLS OF EARLY SETTLEMENT OF THIS REGION AND EXPLOITS OF PIONEERS.

Howard Cessna, Lutzville, Pa., a member of the Bedford, Pa., Kiwanis Club, was the speaker at the noon luncheon-meeting of the Cumberland Kiwanis Club, yesterday at the Fort Cumberland Hotel. Mr. Cessna, a member of the Bedford bar, is a student of colonial history. He gave an account of his research in the early history of this region and the founding of

Fort Cumberland and Fort Bedford, and the pioneer settlers who blazed trails over the Alleghenies. He declared that the settlement of the colonies and the foundation of the present nation was due to the sacrifices and patriotism of the frontiersmen and their women folk.

Mr. Cessna told of the exploits of Augustus Friend, leader of the settlers in the wilderness of what is now Garrett county, Md., and Somerset and Bedford counties in Pennsylvania; how Negro mountain, the highest point in the Alleghenies, was named, after a giant slave who accompanied Friend and was mortally wounded in a fight with the Indians, near its summit.

The speaker gave side-lights and incidents from his search into colonial records, the early traffic over the Nemacolin trail, now the National Highway. He said the infant nation of the United States of America began right in Cumberland, and that no section of the country was so rich in historical possessions.

—*Cumberland, Md. Times, Oct. 1933.*

THE DUNCANSVILLE MEETING—AFTER CESSNA GOT DONE TALKING THE PEOPLE WOULDN'T LISTEN TO MULLIN.

A very successful anti-Thropp mass meeting was held in Duncansville last night. A day or two previous to the holding of the meeting, County Chairman Fox asked Mr. Howard Cessna, of Bedford, under whose direction the affair was arranged, if he would permit a person whom Fox should designate to uphold the Thropp end of the argument. Cessna wished to know who the person was, and when told that it was Mr. W. Scott Mullin, a fellow Bedford countain, he acquiesced. Last evening when Mr. Cessna arrived in Duncansville he was told that the Thropp people had been at work there and had endeavored to keep the best people of the town away from the hall. He was also told that the rougher elements of voters, which would be present, would in all likelihood cause trouble.

When the hour for holding the meeting had arrived fully 300 orderly men had gathered in the town hall. Mr. James Mc-

The House of Cessna

Fadden was elected chairman, and after making a brief address he introduced Hon. Howard Cessna, who held his audience in rapt attention during the entire discourse. Frequently he was interrupted with applause and when he had finished his address he was cheered to the echo.

He said in part:

I believe the Republican principles as taught by Lincoln, Grant, Garfield, Blain and McKinley will live for generations to come. And I believe the custom of sacrificing conscience for party ought to pass away long before this generation ends. This being a Republican form of government, it must be guarded against party spirit and the wiles of political ambition. By our conference system of nominating the voice of the minority may be heard instead of the majority, and when this occurs no true student of this republic will not cry "halt."

Never in the history of this Commonwealth has such a hue and cry come from the Republican party against its own candidate as is now heard here in this Twentieth congressional district.

In the East Side theatre at Altoona, almost two years ago, I told the people of this county that the majority of people in Bedford county were against Mr. Thropp, and I predicted within a few hundred votes, the result that followed.

I now come before you again, this time on a two-fold mission. First to tell you that 2,000 Republicans of our county are not only refusing to vote for Mr. Thropp, but will on the 8th day of this month vote for James M. Walters, of Johnstown. Second, I come to tell you why Mr. Thropp could not carry our county two years ago, why in our last spring's election a majority voted against him, and why Republicans, many of whom have not split their ticket since Abraham Lincoln was assassinated, will vote against him on Tuesday next.

To place myself, however, properly before you, I must say I come not as a disappointed politician, having never been a candidate or an applicant for any office of trust; nor has Quay, Swallow, Wanamaker, Jenks, or any of their henchmen sent me. I come as a volunteer, riding upon no pass, and paying, as I hope to be able, my bills from my own pocket.

I am prompted to do this because, like you, I was taught of the heroic struggles of our ancestors to secure for you and me a home and a government wherein the poorest citizen should have an equal chance in the great battle of life with a millionaire. I was told of Paul Revere's midnight ride, of the death of Nathan Hale, of Webster, Clay, Calhoun, and Lincoln's intellectual struggles, decided by the will of the people, and not by boodle; of each bill of rights in our constitution, costing ages of tears and groans of oppression, and of the going from the north thirty odd years ago of thousands of the first born in so many northern homes, in their love and desire that the humblest citizen may find a home in this republic, where the aristocrats, dukes, lords and millionaires cannot hound the poor man into political oblivion.

Becoming interested in politics, I find citizens of our county, many belonging to the old school, holding up their hands in horror over the political corruption being injected into the politics of Bedford county in order that Mr. Thropp might gratify his desire (as we take it) to get into Washington society; farmers publicly exchanging information as to amount received; meetings by the side of hog-pens, in back alleys, to exchange the amount required; citizens meeting to send a committee to him for boodle; little books recording the names and amounts in the hands of henchmen; followers publicly admitting the use of boodle, and letters from deserted employes, saying they have been in charge of this "pay car" distributing money freely and it is known that he spent $10,000 in his political effort two years ago.

But now I come asking you of Blair county, do you have boys? Are you a poor man? If so what office of trust or honor will you or your children hold if boodle instead of the will of the people is to nominate and elect? Isn't that bringing the question to your own hearthstone? What did the victory at Gettysburg, Shiloh, et. al., mean, if money is to purchase principal and consciousness? Shame to the American republic, if within thirty years the posterity—sons of gallant sires—of the men who wore the blue, have come to admit "there are no honest politicians, that they are all boodlers." If such be true, may heaven in its infinite kindness have mercy on the laboring men of this republic, which was cradled around the hills of Boston and baptized in the blood of the fallen at Yorktown and Appomatox.

This age is calling aloud for the public service of men whose demeanor tells the world they will not sacrifice principle for selfish interest, even though it gains the cheers of the thousands and the praise of the press.

But "boodle" is not the only cause of our opposition to Mr. Thropp. To the minds of many of us, he is void of any milk of kindness in his makeup, when dealing with the poor and beholding class of citizens. I hold in my hand an affidavit that one of his men made, saying he had been discharged because he would not buy more goods at Thropp's company store, etc. This is supported by his clerk's letters, saying "he had positive orders to discharge every man who refused to buy at the store."

I could go on to tell about rent of dwellings for his tenants, suits of labor on justice of the peace dockets, price paid, hours they are expected to work, etc., but I know you read, and the public press has convinced you beyond a doubt.

Men have estimated the amount of boodle Mr. Thropp has spent in Montgomery county and here in his efforts to go to congress as being way up in the tens of thousands. Yet the first pupil I taught in the common schools of our county died a few weeks ago, I am told, before he was able to chance off his watch in order that he could go to the hospital. This little fellow had an arm and leg cut off while working at Thropp's Furnace. A score or more incidents I could refer you to, showing that if this man appreciated the meaning of this republic, boodle could have been more fittingly spent in relieving the distress of his hired men.

Surely the great Captain that kept guard over Lincoln and Grant will not permit party spirit, wealth, aristocracy, aimless society, fine horses and clothes, to befog our minds and elect Thropp over a Christian gentleman, against whom there has not been a Republican paper said aught other than he is a Democrat.

Men of Duncansville, now that the Kentucky boys have

touched elbows with the Green Mountain boys of Vermont, now that the blue and gray have marched together up the hills of San Juan; now that the southern bands not only play "Way Down in Dixie," and "My Maryland," but includes "Three Cheers for the Red, White and Blue," and the "Star Spangled Banner," let us say here in Pennsylvania, on whose soil, by the Delaware, our court was proclaimed, in the City of Brotherly Love our Declaration of Independence was signed; on our soil at Gettysburg, where flowed the best blood of this nation; let us say as Republicans that when a boodler struts among us we, as patriots, drop party and consider first our God, and second our country.

When Cessna had sat down, Mr. Scott Mullin arose and endeavored to refute the statements made against Mr. Thropp, but the audience had been won over to Cessna's side and hissed the gentleman from Hyndman. So great was the confusion that Mullin considered it the better part of valor to remain silent. The meeting was then adjourned. As the crowd dispersed, repeated cheers for Cessna was heard and each one sounded the death knell for Thropp in Duncansville. The Tribune's story that Mullin was prevented from speaking by Cessna, who it alleges turned the lights out, is an invention pure and simple. The people wouldn't listen to Mullin.

—*Altoona Mirror, Nov. 5, 1898.*

MEMORIAL DAY ADDRESS AT COURT HOUSE MARKER

Editor's Note: Address of Howard Cessna, made on the Public Square at Bedford, May 30, 1930, when Marker showing site of first Court House and Jail was unveiled by the Daughters' of the American Revolution which is being published at the request of that organization.

Madame Regent, D. of A. R., Ladies and Gentlemen:

We have come here today to mark the site of the First Court House and Jail that served our ancestors for more than half a century, 1774 to 1829.

This marker has been placed here by the D. of A. R., an organization—nation-wide—comprising three hundred thousand

The House of Cessna

members, who spend hundreds of thousands annually for patriotic education alone; have saved from oblivion the graves of thousands of Revolutionary Soldiers and have marked historical sites over all the Eastern part of this Republic. And this is not all! They have erected the Continental Hall at Washington, their National Headquarters, and have been a leading factor in the present plan to erect the Washington Memorial at Valley Forge which when completed will be the most magnificent Memorial the world around.

They discovered and exposed one thousand papers throughout the land printing Russian propaganda and when a National Atheist's organization attempted to enter our Public Schools, it was immediately combated by the D. of A. R.

In short their motto is: "To perpetuate the names and spirit of our ancestors who made possible our Independence."

In marking historical sites they are aware that the early history of mankind was lost in the night of time; that nothing is known prior to Biblical writing of our English ancestors until Caesar invaded the Island. The same is true of our German ancestors until the Immortal Herman met and conquered the legions of Varnes.

Men of science and wealth are today digging up the Cradle of Mankind—Egypt and India—to learn truths instead of fiction.

Further, America is a new country compared with the Nations of the old world and such patriotic acts as here shown will live for ages.

The D. of A. R. also realizes that it is more than important to mark the steps of progress of our beloved country; for the Infinite Being has emptied the horn of plenty over our land as never shown in the whole history of the world.

With only five per cent of the Earth's area, this Government, created by our forefathers, has acquired two-thirds the gold and the material wealth of the world; we use seven-tenths of the automobiles, radios and telephones of the world; and, in short, the ordinary poor American can live a life of luxury beyond the wildest dream of ancient kings.

Let us hope that this growth has been in keeping with the advice of the Psalmist—"Prosperous be the Nation that worships the true God."

Tradition has it that across the street, either where Mr. Moorehead's residence is, or down at the Barnett building, was erected the first jail which served while the court house and jail were being erected. This was supposed to be a square log building with no doors or windows except a door on top of the roof with a rope ladder that could be drawn out when a prisoner was put in. I presume food and water was served by buckets attached to a rope. Let us hope but few prisoners were incarcerated therein.

The picture shown on this Tablet of the first Court House and Jail has been drawn from memory and given by John Mower, Esq., the artist, while enfeebled by age and ill health.

The building consisted of three stories. The lower one used for the sheriff and prisoners, the second for the court room and the third for the jury rooms.

The only approach to the court room was by means of an outside stairway. The building stood more on the corner of this square than here at this marker. The World War Veterans having made improvements to the front of the Square, with feminine courtesy and wishing to prevent those reading this Tablet from walking over the Legion's grassy plot, the Daughters have chosen this location.

Back of the Court House and Jail extending to the present Lutheran Church was the Jail Yard. In it stood the Whipping Post and Pillory. Court was conducted the first 16 years by three or more Justices of the Peace until 1790 when Judge Thomas Smith, a brother of the Provost of the University of Pennsylvania, presided. He was succeeded by Judges Riddle, Cooper, Jonathan Walker, Huston and last but not least Judge Jno. Todd. Excepting Judges Riddle and Cooper, all of these men were elevated to either a federal Judgeship or to the Supreme Court of Pennsylvania.

Judge Walker lived where the Union Hotel stands and was the father of United States Treasurer Walker whose picture is

The House of Cessna

seen on paper money. Judge Todd lived where the present Post Office stands and in the residence formerly occupied by Moses A. Points, Esq., as a law office. Of him, Judge Hall wrote that Mr. Todd was a Yale graduate and on his first trip to Bedford while at Bloody Run, he was compelled on account of poverty to put up his silk stockings to secure payment for night lodging.

Prior to 1795 the court officers had their offices at various places—the County Commissioners usually meeting at some hotel. In that year just South of the present Gazette building, a building 21x39 feet was erected to accommodate all County officers. After the erection and occupying of our present court house in 1829, these old buildings were allowed to remain until declared a nuisance, when in the early 40's they were removed.

If our first Court House and Jail could appear before a microphone and tell its history, thrill after thrill would be experienced by all who have given consideration to the cost of the Stars and Stripes in our flag.

A moving picture of men ascending the outside steps of the old building, in all probability would show President Washington followed by Generals Allen and Lee of Virginia, 1794; General Arthur St. Clair, our first Prothonotary, whom the artist always pictures as being the only general that Washington kissed good-bye in taking leave of his officers; poor old Col. Crawford whom the Indians tortured to death; Col. Armstrong who put the fear of the white men in the hearts of the Indians at Kittamey as no other save Mad Anthony Wayne, who in all probability also ascended those steps.

Coming down the steps with drawn expression after conference in the Court Room could be seen frontiersmen like Messrs. Martin, Daugherty, Woods, Hugh Barkley, Mann, Davidson and others, excitedly debating whether or not to abandon Bedford as the frontier and all flee to Carlisle; that individual's guns were taken for the army and only 50 pounds of powder left in the County; 35 Tories were found going to Kittaning to coax the Indians to come, kill and scalp their neighbors.

These frontiersmen had been first awed by the French paying $25 per scalp and now same was being repeated by the English. No wonder Thomas Montgomery late State Librarian wrote that, had it not been for the patriotism and sacrifices of the frontiersmen, there would have been no Declaration of Independence nor a United States Constitution; that if you take out of American history the driving out of, first the French, then repelling the Indians and last driving the English out, our history would be commonplace. No spot in America is more hallowed by these events than here around Bedford.

Beyond a doubt, the old Court House and Jail saw many of Capt. Cluggage's men come out of the Indian trails with their round caps and white frocks or rifle shirts.

Unlike the Civil War veterans who entrained at Hopewell, their nearest station, or the World War veterans who entrained here, these Revolutionary soldiers marched to Boston giving an exhibition of marksmanship when passing through New York that few could equal today. While the regiment was on the move they shot at a target, 7 inches square, with their flint lock guns, 250 yards distant, with accuracy.

Many of the frontiersmen were used as sharp-shooters both in the northern and southern campaigns. Nothing brought more good cheer to General Washington in those dark days at Valley Forge, than General Morgan's victory at the battle of Cowpens. Here, frontiersmen on first line of battle with orders to shoot only at officers, the English though numbering two to one, were almost annihilated.

Of course you know that General Jackson later used similar soldiers to defeat Wellington's crack troops, who defeated Napoleon.

If the old jail whose site we mark today could speak, it could tell of Davy Lewis digging out of the dungeon, making his escape, robbing a traveler next day, and, learning a posse was in pursuit, effected a disguise and helped them to hunt himself. It could tell of some harsh sentences inflicted on wrong doers. A horse thief received 25 lashes, both ears cut off and nailed to the pillory in which he was placed.

Yes, it is by marking just such historical sites that true history is preserved and it is hoped that this marker will serve to

The House of Cessna

not only teach the present but on-coming generations of the sacrifices and patriotism shown by the frontiersmen who built and used this building.

Let us hope our country will continue to move on and upward to that condition of which statesmen have dreamed and poets have sung.   —*Bedford Gazette, Jan. 1931.*

Home, 1, 28, 1931

Howard Cessna Esq.

Dear Sir and Friend: I procured a copy of the Gazette containing your address and was very interested in its reading. I would congratulate you on the attractive form of the address and the pleasing way of reciting our history.

I did not look for error of figure or facts as you have stated them, except Daniel Palmer was threshed more for horse stealing than you say, 39 lashes instead of 25. He probably counted more correctly than we now estimate.

Your address will henceforth appear in my valued scrap book.

E. Howard Blackburn.

CLASS HISTORY, 1932

"Sitting alone by the way-side, sat a hoary Pilgrim; 'Stranger,' says he, 'we are growing old'." So are we, and the only comfort I get is: we are rid of many silly notions entertained by youth. "Much water has run under the Bridge in forty years." Here is hoping for another forty years for us all.

"We pass this way but once. Only actors on the stage, then we pass on." I've often thought it's a pity we can't live our life the second time. If we could and the Faculty was the same as in 1892, I would, without hesitation, pack my trunk for Millersville. I love its memory and think if one did not make good, it was not the fault of Miss Lyle, Prof. Byerly, Dr. Hull, Prof. Roddy, Miss Gilbert and Dr. Lyte. Thirty years ago, in company with the Dan Webster of our county, we attended a picnic and made speeches. On our way home I said, "I'll appreciate if you criticize my speech." In reply he said, "The American people are too smart to allow anyone to talk of self. Never attempt it and expect attention."

However a Class History I take it, is an exception, hence here goes:

My life since I parted with you has been successful, if by success you mean health and contentment. I've been what a friend called me when introducing me at a public meeting in our Court House—"A Farmer Lawyer." From this you observe, I've been riding two horses going in opposite directions. I've not set the creek afire in either avocation but I assure you I've had my fling without the extreme worry and tension that follows the exacting professional. Until I was fifty years of age, I remained a bachelor, having my parents, brothers and sisters to care for me, or as a friend might put it—caring for them. It was July 2, 1921, when I married and now after eleven years of married life, I'm sorry I did not marry about fifty-one years earlier.

If I were to select some outstanding achievement in life after leaving Normal it would be my success in disposing of real estate. I owned and sold to the State around 16,000 acres of mountain land, and best of all, since the depression, I had wished on me four farms due to becoming security for others—and these I unloaded without loss to myself. In my efforts to sell my land to the State, I frequently surveyed, living in a tent on the mountain just for short periods. In this out-door experience I must have unrolled ancestral traits for I secured a pack of thoroughbred fox hounds, killing ten foxes in eight hunts. My sisters from the city gave me curtain calls to such an extent, I gave the hounds away and did not hunt for twenty years until last fall when I helped to kill five deer in two days on my own land. Like Washington, a dance and a hunt appeal to me strongly. But do not take this so literally as to infer I've neglected real endeavor in life. I give this only as information as to life's background since we all sang "God be with you until we meet again."

I take it that in an article like Class History is wanted an

The House of Cessna

individual's account of one's self. Without any attempt at boasting in that line, may I add that I discover in my past, a qualification that places me ahead of Abraham Lincoln. He was defeated three times for Congress before being elected. I've been defeated five times and never elected. I have it all over the martyr. Once for District Attorney, twice for the Legislature and twice for Congress. I console myself with Shakespeare's idea that "Victory is not always with the strong." My political success has largely been determined by not putting boodle into my campaigns. For instance on one occasion my sole contribution was a two-cent stamp to mail my nomination papers. I always carried handsomely my home district, being unlike Bob Ingersol, who said he always ran best where he was not known. You know that if Miss Lyle were alive, she would say that Judge Coolidge claimed the greatest canker gnawing at the American fabric was lynch law and money in politics.

I have but one little regret when I think of my school days. It's this: I am sorry I did not know that the taproots of my people who bore me was in generations gone by, intimately associated with the early days of Chester, Lancaster, York and Cumberland Counties. Just why frontier fever should bring my ancestors out of Carlisle into the more rugged County of Bedford has remained a puzzle. However, don't take that as a slap at Bedford County, for liberty has always found her warmest supporters from the lands and the lassies who dwell by the mountain side. Further, don't judge Bedford County solely by views from the Lincoln Highway, as we have coves and valleys rivaling in soil, fertility and up-to-date farms with the best in the State. Again apologizing for self praise, allow me to add that the farm on which I was born has the best barn in Bedford County, receiving at times one thousand dollars per month from milk alone, and has been in the Cessna family for six generations. Those of you who were caught in the 1929 Stock Market crash need not get green in the eye, as my farm on which I live in the summer is not that farm.

Webster said the first thing to know in speech making was when to sit down. For fear I tire you, I'm ending with this request. Since graduation, I've seen but three of my classmates—Bill Dill, Walter Noble and Miss Wertz. Any of you passing through Bedford, please locate me, and better yet, if it's summer, come out into Friends Cove to my country home and visit me. Our ancestors had to pull the Latch String in to lock out enemies. You will find my Latch String on the outside to any Millersvillian.

———

October 20, 1927.

Mr. Howard Cessna, Esq.,
  Bedford, Pennsylvania.

Dear Sir: On behalf of the Pennsylvania Daughters of the American Revolution, may I extend to you our gratitude and appreciation for bringing to us such a worth while message from our brother organization, the Sons of the American Revolution.

It would not seem like a State Conference unless we had greetings from your Society, and again I wish to thank you.

Cordially yours,
Mary B. Arrowsmith,
(Mrs. Joseph B.)
State Corresponding Secretary.

June 21, 1932.

Howard Cessna, Esq.,
  Lutzville, Pa.

My dear Mr. Cessna: We wish to thank you for your part in helping to make the Washington Memorial Exercises at Sideling Hill a success. You certainly gave an interesting and wonderful address and I am still hearing many a complimentary remark about it.

Very truly yours,
H. B. Phillips,
District Forester.

The House of Cessna

MY EXPERIENCE AS A ROAD VIEWER

For the past twenty years I've been Attorney for the Board of Road Viewers which is, on a guess, five times longer than any other member of whom I have knowledge. I never asked for the appointment. When my term expired years ago, the Associate Judge who was my cousin, S. A. Cessna, called me on the phone to tell me his first act as Judge was to reappoint me and in jocular mood said "I should now send on his turkey." To this I replied I'd cheerfully give him a turkey if he'd not appoint me.

However, I've been reappointed all these years and my duties have taken me into every nook and corner of the county many times. Without any exception the crowds that assembled at the Views were always friendly with us even if they were out of tune with one another. In a county like Lancaster I'm told the work is almost constant and one would be recompensed nicely. Here the job some years has not been worth fifty dollars.

By reason of notices having to be up ten days in advance, it's a guess as to the kind of weather. We have run into all descriptions. To survey an old road, say three miles long, on a hot August day or to lay out a new one through the brush on a cold winter day is not a luxury.

On no occasion have we ever been offered a bribe and I've never served with a Viewer whom I thought would accept one if offered. Always the law forbids our accepting any free dinner, lunch, etc., and this was always adhered to. We came near to stepping over the traces once.

A new farmer—a city farmer—had his wife prepare us a dinner, knowing we'd be about his place at noon. When we arrived an invitation was sent to call us to dinner. I told the party we could not accept unless they'd take pay. This was refused, so we were preparing to go a couple miles to a restaurant when a Caretaker struck on the plan of selling us sandwiches, which when eaten he would accept nothing but twenty-five cents. Later the owner had a laugh over that twenty-five cents, saying it was the first money he had received from his farm.

After finishing the surveys the return trip was generally enlivened by swapping stories mostly the kind that Lincoln excused himself from listening to, by saying he enjoyed them not for rough part, but for the wit and humor.

In my last and first road view I saw a display of temper beyound any other. I was ordered off a man's lot with threats of bodily harm and then dared out in the road, where I went expecting to defend myself. To my agreeable surprise when I got to the road he called my attention to a tile his neighbor had removed, thus giving the crowd and particularly me, a chance to cool off. I never saw such a display or hysterical show of temper.

My first View was on a private road view. The parties were brother-in-laws. After hearing both sides and viewing the grounds, I told them life was up hill enough for all of us and if they got me pen and ink I'd write an agreement between them and give my days fee of $5.00 to both if they'd sign. The one agreed, the other with an oath said he'd never. So on went the view and with it, three fights, two of them, if not all three, ended in Court.

One was an old pupil of mind and thinking this would have some influence over me was desirous of getting a private talk. He had just been hit with brass knuckles by the side of his face and being much over six feet tall and nervous from his fight, attempted to touch me on the shin with the toe of his boot to attract my attention. He attracted it alright, for he barked my shin from top to bottom.

Real early in my experience as a Viewer, I discovered the Court had permitted the Board to adopt a set of rules that permitted the whole Board meeting in Bedford and charging for the day if they had business or not. My first attendance broke up this plan as I refused to charge for the day as there was no work to be done. Had this custom continued until now, thousands of dollars in tax funds would have gone.

I presume by reason of my being an old member of the Board, the County Convention of Supervisors call on me annually to address them. During my time on the Board death has

The House of Cessna

removed the following: George Cunnard, George Blackburn, David Prosser, Levi Smith, Elbert C. Weaverling, Squire J. M. Imler, Evans, Daniel Shuss, Barton Jay, Lewis Pittman, W. H. Weyant.

Occasionally—not often—Viewers have had schemes practiced to deceive them. If a few citizens did not want an old road vacated, just before the View, the old road not used but a couple times in the past ten years would become all marked up with wagon and auto tracks.

In desiring a new road, some ingenious fellow with an old car would get ahead of the other cars and in order to impress the Viewers with the supposed steep grade, would purposely stall his car and all hands called to help out.

The following have served on the Board and their time either expired, else they resigned: Stanley Blackburn, Walter Madore, Lincoln Shroyer, Hayes Cunnard, Squire Fluck.

The present Viewers: Elten Lee, Surveyor; Howard Roudabush, Surveyor; E. M. Pennell, Esq., H. Wesley Holler, Howard Cessna, Esq., John T. Matt, Albert R. Layton, E. E. Mills, Joseph Wambaugh, John Lawhead, Norman Mower.

HOWARD CESSNA

Height 5 feet, 11 inches; age, 63 years, when this Book was published; eyes, blue; hair, dark brown; weight around 180 lbs.

MILITARY RECORD

Too old to have taken part in World War, but right age for Spanish War. While practicing law at Everett, formerly called "Bloody Run," I was chosen Captain of a company and at my own expense had Major Mickle of Pennsylvania Nation Guard drill us.

The Spaniards must have learned we were from Bloody Run, as they sued for peace before we got into the service, hence military records went glimmering. What a record!

From my observation the prevailing characteristics of the Cessnas are dark hair, brown eyes and a leaning towards dark complexion, some showing French. However, when science tells us on the one line of descent since America was discovered, we have 16 ancestors, and from the earlier European line—possible 16,000. One is apt to expect most any and every physical characteristic that might be imagined.

Dec. 18, 1933.

CHAPTER XVI

Letters from Mrs. Beck, Mt. Pleasant, Mich. and
Mrs. Morgan, Ames, Iowa

Mount Pleasant, Mich., Feb. 25, 1935.

Dear Mr. Cessna: It might be well to introduce myself before telling the mission of this letter. I am the daughter of John Elwood Miller of Buffalo Mills and Jennie Stuckey of Wolfsburg.

I am a Daughter of the American Revolution and used the name of John Cessna as my ancestor who served in the war.

I understand that you have a coat of arms of the Cessna family. Will you kindly tell me how to procure one of these and what the cost is? I should like so much to have one and will appreciate this information greatly.

Very truly yours,
Mae Miller Beck.

2225 Knapp St., Ames, Iowa, Aug. 2, 1934.

Mr. Howard Cessna,
  Bedford, Pa., R. D. 4.

Dear Mr. Cessna: I am enclosing a check for $2.00 for a new addition to, or rather new edition of, House of Cessna. I shall be much interested in it.

Did I send you a statement of the death of my father, O. H. Cessna? To be sure, I am sending another copy.

There is no other news of our immediate family except the marriage of our daughter, Catharine Cessna Morgan to William Duncan Giffen on June 6, 1933. They are living at Glidden, Wisconsin.

Anything I can do to help the cause along will be done most cheerfully.

Very truly yours,

Ethyl Cessna Morgan
(Mrs. C. M. Morgan).

CHAPTER XVII

Obituaries

DR. ORANGE HOWARD CESSNA

AMES, IA.—On the grounds of the college he served for 30 years, the body of Dr. Orange Howard Cessna, 79, Iowa State college chaplain, will be buried Tuesday.

Funeral services will be held in the great hall of the memorial union at 2:30 p. m., and the body will be buried beside that of his wife and his son—in the college cemetery.

Dr. Cessna died Saturday, having served the college for 30 years. He was a member of the school's first graduating class, and had spent the last 75 years in central Iowa.

Dr. Cessna was dictating a letter to a stenographer in a room of the Memorial Union, where he lived, when he was stricken.

He became chaplain of the college in 1902 and still taught a few classes at the time of his death.

Dr. Cessna, chaplain and instructor in pyschology and religion, was one of the best known members of the faculty of Iowa State college.

Although his daily life brought him in contact with many college students, he was not discouraged about the trend of modern youth. The controversy between science and religion did not greatly disturb him. He accepted scientific truths and anticipated the liberalizing of religious thought.

He was born in Kenton, Ohio, July 31, 1852. When he was 4, his parents moved to Nevada, Ia.

At 16, Mr Cessna entered Iowa State college when that institution consisted of one building. He joined the Crescent Literary and the Bachelor Debating societies.

Mr. Cessna supported himself while in college by milking cows and by teaching during a portion of the year. For a time

DR. ORANGE HOWARD CESSNA

after graduation he worked as a bookkeeper in a general store at Iowa Center.

He attended Garret Biblical institute and Northwestern university at Evanston, Ill. After being ordained he had several parishes in Illinois.

In 1900 he returned to Iowa State college as head of the history and psychology departments. In 1924, at his own request, he was relieved of the responsibility as head of the departments, but continued to teach classes in child psychology, and the social and ethical teachings of the Apostles and Christ. He also was made college chaplain.

STEPHEN S. CISNEY

Stephen S. Cisney, resident of Coleridge and the nearby community for 40 years, died Monday evening with his wife and all their children at his bedside in his dying moments. Death came as a climax to a brief illness during which Mr. Cisney suffered a paralytic stroke and other complications which hastened his passing.

Funeral services for the well-known resident were held yesterday afternoon from the home and later at the Methodist church of which he was a member. Rev. R. F. Farley, pastor of the Coleridge and Belden churches, presided over the services at the church and the interment rites in the Coleridge cemetery.

Mr. Cisney was born in Solsbury, Indiana, on January 4, 1858, and continued to lived at his birth place until he was 18 years old, when he moved to Lafayette, Illinois. On February 23, 1879, he married Miss Marjorie J. Stephens of Newark, Indiana. Following their marriage the couple lived for a year in Illinois, moving to Aurelia, Iowa, where they spent the next four years. Following six years in Brown County, Nebraska, they came to Cedar County where they have continued to reside. Until 1917 they farmed north of town. Since their retirement they have lived in their present residence.

The golden wedding anniversary of Mr. and Mrs. Cisney was the occasion for a happy family gathering on February 23,

1929. Mr. Cisney was a charter member of the Belden and Coleridge Odd Fellow lodges whose members had charge of the funeral arrangements. He was active in lodge work and had a large circle of friendship in which he was a popular figure.

He is survived by his widow who cared for him during the brief illness which preceded his death: six sons, Earl, Sidney, Ernest and Kinley of Coleridge and Arlie and Joe of Nehawka; two daughters, Mrs. Fred Gibson of Holstein, Iowa, and Mrs. Will Roberts of Randolph; and 38 grandchildren and five great-grandchildren. He also leaves two sisters who are Mrs. Harriet Duncan of Bloomington, Ind., and Mrs. Agnes Ingle of Pateau, Oklahoma.

JOHN CALVIN CESSNA

John Calvin Cessna president of the Cessna-Magruder automobile finance company and vice-president of the Buley-Patterson Company, merchandise brokers, died suddenly last night at 7 o'clock from a heart attack at his home, 225 Bedford street. He was 57 years old.

Mr. Cessna was a native of Cumberland and a life-long resident. He was a member of the Board of Directors of the Cumberland Fair Association and designer and supervisor of the traffic system which enabled the Fair Association to handle the huge crowds which attended the organization's race meeting and exposition in the past three years. He was a charter member of the Cumberland Rotary Club.

Mr. Cessna was also prominent in the Masonic fraternity, a member of Potomac Lodge No. 100, A. F. & A. M.; a member of Cumberland Consistory, A. & A. Scottish Rite Bodies; a member of Temple Ali Ghan, A. A. O. Nobles of the Mystic Shrine, and a member of the advisory board of the Order of De-Molay. He was also a member of the United Commercial Travelers of America.

Besides his wife, Mrs. Jane Grey Cessna, Mr. Cessna is survived by one son, Holmes H. Cessna, with whom he is associated in business, and by one brother, William F. Cessna, Altoona, Pa.

ALFRED J. CISNEY

Alfred J. Cisney, a former resident of Pittsburgh, died Sunday night in his home in Richmond Hill, N. Y., according to word received here yesterday. He was born in Pennsylvania and had resided in Pittsburgh many years. While in this city he was connected with the real estate department of the Commonwealth Trust Company. He moved to Richmond Hill 19 years ago and had been engaged in the real estate business in that place. He leaves his wife, Mrs. Maud Pipes Cisney; two sons, William and Delbert Cisney, and two daughters, Miss Gladys and Miss Luella Cisney, at home.—*Bedford Gazette, Feb. 16, 1926.*

LORENZO DOWE CESSNA

Lorenzo Dowe Cessna, one of the most prominent farmers of Cumberland Valley, died this morning at 8:15 o'clock. The funeral will take place from the Methodist Protestant church at Centerville, on Wednesday at 10 o'clock, Rev. Howard L. Schlincke officiating. The interment will be made at Bethel cemetery. The deceased leaves one son, Duncan Cessna, who lives on the home farm, and one daughter, Allie, who is married to Forrest Snowden, and lives at Mayview, Missouri. He also leaves one brother, Weaver B. Cessna, and one sister, Mrs. John A. Wertz, who live in Cumberland Valley. His age was 70 years, 10 months and 9 days. Mr. Cessna was noted for his hospitality and was always pleased to have people visit him. The latch string was always out to everybody.

JUDGE J. B. CESSNA

Judge J. B. Cessna, 88 years old, an attorney, passed away in his home, 104 West Linwood boulevard, yesterday, after a five weeks' illness.

Judge Cessna formerly held a judicial post in Nebraska. He was active in Mexican land grant cases taken before the United States supreme court. A case in which he acted as counsel had its inception in courts in 1819.

A resident of Erie, Pa., from 1905 to 1925, Judge Cessna then moved to Kansas City.

Survivors are: the widow, Mrs. Catherine U. Cessna; and two sons, W. E. Cessna, Council Bluffs, Ia., and Reon B. Cessna, 7412 Flora avenue.—*Kansas City Journal, Jan. 14, 1928.*

THOMAS R. CESSNA

Thomas R. Cessna died at his home at Grinnel, Ia., on Sunday, March 26, aged 83 years. 4 months and 29 days.

Mr. Cessna was born in Friend's Cove, near Rainsburg, on October 27, 1827, and was a son of William and Rachael Cessna. He moved west about half a century ago where for years he was engaged in farming and the real estate business, though for some years prior to his death he had lived retired. He is survived by two brothers, William Cessna of Rainsburg and J. Boone of Erie, and the following children: Mrs. Laura Burnsides, Mrs. Ella Van Evera, Newton W., Mrs. Belle Robison, John T., Mrs. Hattie Jacobs and Mrs. Myrtle Porage, all of Iowa.

About seven years ago Mr. Cessna spent some time in this section visiting his relatives and former acquaintance.—*Bedford Gazette, March 31, 1911.*

MRS. PHILIP A. BARNETT

Mrs. Clara C. Barnett died at her home in Saxton, Thursday, April 27. She was born in this county May 31, 1870, a daughter of Weaver B. and Mary Anne (Snowden) Cessna. Surviving are her husband, Philip A. Barnett, and two sons, Eugene of Bedford and William of Saxton; also, four brothers and seven sisters: Stephen of Pittsburgh, John and L. D. of Chicago and Howard of Rt. 3, Bedford; Mrs. Fannie Carpenter, Oklahoma City, Okla.; Mrs. Ella Wertz, Cleveland, O.; Mrs. Florence Brubaker, Chicago; Mrs. Myrtle Lightner, Marysville; Mrs. J. B. Lobingier of Pittsburgh; Mrs. Harry Hummer, Latrobe, and Mrs. J. M. Fink, Saxton.

MRS. HELEN CESSNA DOUGHERTY

The death of Mrs. Helen Cessna Dougherty, one of the pioneer and most remarkable women of this county occurred at 5:30 last evening at her home on North Detroit street.

Mrs. Dougherty was nearly ninety years of age—the exact age being 88 years, two months and four days. She was the mother of one of the county's most prominent families and a lady highly reverenced by all who knew her.

Helen Cessna Dougherty was the eldest of ten children of Jonathan and Catherine (Boore) Cessna who came from Bedford, Cumberland Co., Pa., in the year 1831. Helen Cessna was born at New Bedford, Nov. 13th, 1821. She was 4 years old when her parents left that state for Coshocton, Ohio. After a residence there for a while, Jonathan Cessna moved his family to Hardin county and settled on a tract of 714 acres near Ft. McArthur, part of the land being still owned by one of the Cessnas 1½ miles west of Kenton.

Jonathan Cessna was one of the big men of this part of the state. In 1832 he was associate judge, and in 1842 was elected judge for a period of seven years by the Ohio Assembly. Helen Cessna, while attending a private academy in Kenton, first met William Dougherty and they wedded here Dec. 13, 1849. William Dougherty, who was a prominent merchant of this city, died June 2, 1887.

William and Helen Dougherty were the parents of five children, three of whom survive, Attorney James W. Dougherty, Kate May, and Howard Dougherty, all of Kenton. The eldest child was the Hon. Frank C. Dougherty whose death occurred in this city, June 8, 1908. The fifth child, Charles, died in infancy.

Of the brothers and sisters of Helen Dougherty the following survive: Jonathan Wilson Cessna of California; Oliver Perry Cessna of Arkansas; Mrs. Harriet Cessna Moore of Nebraska; Dr. Benjamin Franklin Cessna and Col. William T. Cessna of Kenton.

The deceased was united with the First Methodist Episcopal

church in 1838. She had been a resident of the county since 1831, and a resident of Kenton since 1849. When her family moved here the site of Kenton was nothing but a wilderness; and during her life she witnessed that wilderness transformed into a large thriving city, and the county transformed into one of the most productive of a great state.

Mrs. Dougherty had been in remarkably good health, but at the death of her brilliant son a year and a half ago the shock of grief had a noticeable effect. However she retained all of her splendid faculties until the end. About five weeks ago the final fatal illness made its appearance. It was heart trouble superinduced by senility that caused her demise. The end came in peace and glory at 5:30 last evening.

The funeral service will be held at the late home Wednesday beginning at 1:30 p. m. The Rev. E. E. McCammon will officiate; and the burial will be made in Grove cemetery.

Mrs. Dougherty was a woman of unusually bright intellect and overflowing charms. Even in her old age she was vigorous, and hearty, and took an active interest in the affairs of life until touched by the hand of death. She was a well informed reader, and until the last read the latest magazines and papers and took the keenest interest in current events and issues. She was one of those brilliant women of the past living with us in the present. A good conversationalist and of rare graciousness she enjoyed entertaining her friends at her home and looking after their comfort there as in the sprightliness of youth. Educated and of refined nature, and possessing so many admirable traits of heart, mind and soul, Mrs. Dougherty was indeed a remarkable character, and her departure leaves a vacancy that is keenly felt.

With all these virtues it is truthfully said her goodness of heart was yet her greatest charm. Charitable she was to the needy but charitable in a quiet way. She won by her own good graces, the life long regard and devotion of many loving friends. Her death is a loss to the community. She was one of those last passing pioneers that linked the early history of our community with the present. She was one of those beautiful characters that have left their ineffable impress upon the community, to such a degree that, although she is passed away, we may yet say she lives with her friends still. Her life was a beautiful Christian. Her years were full and fruitful. The glory of her life and the peacefulness of the eventide go to console the otherwise sad and heavy hearts of relatives and many friends.—*From News Republican, Kenton, Ohio, Jan., 1910.*

DR. BENJAMIN FRANKLIN CESSNA

Dr. Benjamin Franklin Cessna, a retired physician and one of Kenton's most prominent citizens was found dead in bed Sunday morning at his home on North Detroit Street, where he resided. Dr. Cessna was found by Dr. A. R. Grove, who resides in separate apartments of the house in which Dr. Cessna resided. The discovery was made about 10:00 o'clock after the members of the Grove family had become alarmed at not hearing Dr. Cessna arise as usual in the morning.

The aged man was found reclining on the bed, where he had fallen, it is presumed, after attempting to arise. It is thought that the doctor had been up, for he had on his slippers and had grown ill suddenly and sat down on the edge of the bed. When found his one hand was holding his other wrist as though he was feeling his pulse. It is presumed that death came between six and seven o'clock. Death was due to gas on the stomach which affected the heart.

There was something unusually pathetic and singularly interesting about the last few hours of this eccentric and venerable man. Dr. and Mrs. Grove had noticed that lately Dr. Cessna had not been in his usual good health. They spoke to him about his health and asked him to let them know if he became ill in the night.

On the last day of the old year Dr. Cessna went into the Grove home, and spoke of the dying year in reference to his own life.

"This is the last day of 1910" spoke Mr. Cessna, "I am liable to pass on and up most any time. I may not be here in 24 hours, I don't want to go, but I am liable to go." He never spoke of dying, he always referred to death as "passing on and up." Later that day he met Mrs. Grove who wished him a happy new year and in reply came Dr. Cessna's last words, "Mrs. Grove I wish you a very happy new year, a doubly happy one."

He passed on into his adjoining room and a few minutes later Mrs. Grove seated herself at the piano and played for him, that he could hear in his adjoining room. He loved music. It was for this reason that when the Grove family moved in the house last fall and learning that Mrs. Grove could play the piano, he purchased one and presented it to Mrs. Grove. He afterwards said that, this gift had given him more happiness than any other thing he ever did.

It was thus on the evening of the last day of the old year that he sat in his room listening to the music he loved and the last piece Mrs. Grove played was "Jesus Lover of My Soul."

The next morning Mrs. Grove, somewhat worried and still remembering what Dr. Cessna had said on the day before, was annoyed at not hearing him arise as usual. So she seated herself before the piano and sought to arouse him with the strains of "The Holy City," but the music fell on ears that even then were stilled in death. It was an hour or so later that Mr. Grove entered the room by taking out a window.

Dr. Cessna came to this county with his parents when but seven years old. He was born in the Cumberland Valley, near Bedford Springs, Pennsylvania Jan. 26, 1826. In 1833 the Cessna family came to Hardin county, landing here on the third day of May. The family was an influential one in the pioneer community and for twelve years Mr. Cessna's father served as associate judge.

"Dr. Cessna grew up with the energies and ambitions of the great west and soon mastered the learning of the local schools within his reach. Like many another young American he then became a school master; but his thirst for knowledge was not yet satisfied. In 1864 he entered the Ohio Wesleyan University from which he was later graduated and later still received the Master's degree. He completed a medical course in the University of Michigan, receiving his diploma in 1852. After six years of successful practice the young physician entered the Jefferson Medical School at Philadelphia and received his degree from that institution in 1858.

In 1855 Dr. Cessna began the practice of medicine in Van Wert until 1876.

In his profession and also in his investments he was successful, the passing years bringing him as result of his well directed efforts not only comfort and plenty but a competency from which he has drawn liberally and from time to time made gifts to numerous worthy causes. He was elected a trustee of the Ohio Wesleyan University. He deeded to that institution property sufficient to provide for a professorship. The income of the property goes to the University and provides for the perpetual maintenances of a chair of English language and literature which bears his name in the college. Dr. Cessna was the second graduate of the college thus to provide for the endowment of a chair. Besides this Dr. Cessna gave much to other charities.

On retiring from the practice of medicine in 1876, he came to Kenton conducting his farms near the city, where he has since made his home. In the meantime he has visited extensively. In 1884 he visited Europe and in 1902 he went to Palestine and visited the different countries on the Mediterranean Sea. He visited Egypt and went up the Nile, and also visited Greece.

Deceased is survived by two brothers Col. W. T. Cessna of Sandusky City and Wilson Cessna of Orange, California, and one sister, Mrs. Henry Moore of Long Pine, Nebraska.

Dr. Cessna was a Royal Arch Mason and a member of the Alumni association of the University of Michigan. The funeral will be held from the Dougherty home on North Detroit Street, Tuesday at 1:30 p. m. Mrs. Dougherty whose death occurred about a year ago was a sister.—*From Kenton, Ohio, Daily, Jan. 2, 1911.*

CHAPTER XVIII

French History of Cessna's

De La Chesnaye Des Bois: (Dictionary of Nobility)
Paris, 1770-1786, Volume IV, P. 29

Cesne or *Sesne-de Menilles* (le) in Normandy: Lá Roque in his "History of the House of Harcourt, pages 512, 1316, 1869 and 1994, makes mention of one William Le Cesne, Chaplain and Secretary to the King of France, who had replevin of this temporalities from the King of England Henry Vth., in 1521; one Jean le Cesne, who, on the 26th, December 1373, shared an inheritance, coming from Jean de Boissey, jointly with Roger de Murdrac, Bernard de la Tour, Jean de Fontaines and Jean Tirel; and one Louise le Cesne, wife of James le Conte, Baron de Nonant, Lord de Cernieres, son of Charles le Conte and of Catherine d'Anfreville. He was widower of her in 1529, and he remarried Bonne d'Espinay-de-Saint-Luc.-Coat of Arms: Quarter, argent and gules.

Paris, January 15, 1935

Dear Sir: After despatching my last letter to you, I received a communication from one of my foreign correspondents, calling my attention to the coat-of-arms of a Northern Italy family named Cesana.

This coat-of-arms, which please find in the margin hereof, is absolutely identical with that figuring on the cover-page of your pamphlet.

From this it would appear that this pamphlet, while referring to the name of Cesne, in point of text (page 13), refers to the name Cesana as to the coat-of-arms.

Your problem thus becomes a double one: You descent

The House of Cessna

either from the Cesne family of Normandy or from the Cesana family. They are utterly different families. However your name more closely resembles the Cesana one.

Do you happen to have family papers (seal, engraving, etc.) bearing coat-of-arms, or in fact particulars of any kind which would lead to suppose your connexion rather with the Cesne family than with the Cesanas or vice versa.

With the expression of my regard,

Very truly yours,

J. S. Willems.

Brussels, January 12, 1935.

Dear Sir: I.—The searches made in France regarding the origin and existence of the Cessna Family, have proved that formerly both the forms Cesne and Sesne are to be met with in the same deeds and that the families are, therefore identical.

I am saying "families," not yet being in the position to state positively that there only one and the same family concerned. In my opinion, the meaning of the surname "le Cesne" would be "le Chene" (old French "le Chesne") in English "the Oak," in which case, it would be a question of a common name becoming a proper name.

II.—So far as the results to date warrant that conclusion, the Cesnes in all their mode spelling are chiefly met with in Normandy and in Touraii, its neighbour, whose centers are the cities of Rouen, Alencon and Tours.

III.—I have not thought fit, for the time being at least, to be concerned about the spellings Cyresnes, Ciresnes which appear to deviate too far from our spellings, which are in fact other names. But I have noted the Cesneau and Cesnet spellings, which are ancient forms of Cesnes.

I have found nothing under the forms of Cesnin, Cesna, Cesine, Cesena. On the other hand, a certain old table refers from the name of Carducene back to the name of Cesne.

IV.—I have dealt with three groups of records, namely:

(a) Coats-of-arms registered by Hozier, herald of arms of France, by order of the King of France Louis XIV, in 1697; these documents still exist at the present day and are absolutely authentic.

It must be remembered that above registration included the recording the armorial bearings of the noblemen, burghers, persons, abbeys, cities, communes, craftsmen's corporations, etc. This registration was not altogether compulsory, though most of the persons interested subjected to it.

The appendix hereto reproduces all the data found in connection with the names of Cesne and Sesne in the Hozier registers.

I notice that not one of these armorial bearings agrees with the blazon—heraldically incomplete be it said—ornamenting the cover of the little book you sent me.

(b) I have been through a whole lot of French archives and have found documents—some on parchment, others on paper—mostly very ancient and among them papers such as genealogical sketches, very important. There are, roughly speaking, one hundred pages of text with olverse and reverse.

(c) Lastly, I have noted in other genealogical and historical documentary Collections, a further large number of references which I have not yet examined and with whose importance, either as to quantity or quality, I am therefore still unacquainted but which, considering the nature of these records, would certainly be interesting.

I may add that I have limited my investigations to the collections kept in Paris. This means that I have not dealt with archives lying elsewhere, namely in Normandy, whose documentary value should not be under-rated.

I enclose, herewith, the armorial bearings found, hoping that Mr. Cessna, after comparing them with his own data, will be able to determine what sources, names and places should chiefly be searched.

I would suggest dealing in the first instance, with group (b) above and this in the most simple and practical way, by reproducing the pages by photostates.

The House of Cessna

In this preparatory investigation, I have not thought it necessary to consult La Roque's treatise to which the Dictionary of Nobility refers. However, the enclosed photostate, representing page 79 of this Dictionary, shows to what extent the text quoted on page 13 of your pamphlet is incomplete and inaccurate.

As stated in this letter, the armorial bearings indicate by the Dictionary correspond to those found by me, but not to those appearing on the cover of the pamphlet.

Searches and work to-date represent, disbursements included, the sum of 1500 francs viz. 150.—Dutch Florins; in order to simplify matters, I should be obliged if you would remit this amount to my account at the "Rotterdamsche Bankvereeniging" at The Hague (Holland), through an American Bank.

With respect to the name Schomberg and the Battle of the Boyne, I attach herewith in photostates, 3 biographies taken from various European books. I did not have these texts translated into English, not knowing whether these translations were required and wishing to avoid unnecessary labour and expense. However, I have the texts at hand and I can always supply these translations on request.

At the end of these articles, are lists of references. On my part, I have other titles of works. All this could be examined.

Please tell me also whether in future, ancient text to be taken in photostates as mentioned above, or generally speaking, other texts, are to be recopied in modern writing and translated into English.

In conclusion, I think I am correct in saying that the case of Cessna—Cesne in Europe is an interesting one and that in all probability, useful results can be anticipated.

As regard the continuation of the work, I shall wait Mr. Cessna's instructions.

With the expression of my regard,

Yours very truly,

J. S. Willems.

Brussels, July 7, 1934.

Dear Sir: I am in receipt of your letter to which I hasten to reply.

When next I am passing through France, I will investigate the historical question of the Cessnas and that according to the directions contained in your letters and in the lines of my last letter to you.

It is not possible to quote charges for this prior examination, but I will enclose an account of same with the result of this first enquiry and you can be assured it will not ruin you.

I was forgetting to tell you, in reply to the P. S. to your letter of June 18th, that I find in France two places called by the name of Cesny: (1) Cesny aux Vignes (the Vines), and (2) Cesny-Bois-Halbout, also called Cesny en Cinglais, both being hamlets in the Calvados, each counting some 500 inhabitants.

I do not believe that these names have anything in common with the Cessna family.

I suppose you are alluding to the History of the Duke of Schomburg generally and not to any particular History which may have been published and which I could look up in our Libraries here.

With best regards,
I am, dear Sir,
Yours very truly,
J. S. Willems.

Brussels, May 17, 1934

Dear Sir: Your letter of the 4th ultimo has had my due attention.

The preparatory investigation which I have made leads to the following conclusions:

(1) Upwards of 35 years experience has taught me that, in crossing the Ocean, names of families coming from our continent to settle in America have, as a rule, undergone more or less transformations in the way of spelling.

That is the case with the name "Cessna," which is not of

The House of Cessna

French form (double "s" followed by "n" and final "a" being unknown in the French language).

(2) Not once have the numerous and important onomastic French indexes shown the following forms:

Ces(s)na, Ses(s)na, Ces(s)ina, Ces(s)ena.

On the other hand, there exist, more particularly in Touraine and Normandy, numerous references to the names of Cesne, le Cesne, Cesene, Cesneau, Cesnet, Sesne, le Sesne and le Ceine.

(3) The Pamphlet "Tablet" which you forwarded me, state on page 13 the spelling Cisne. I have failed to find anywhere this form of Cisne, and the like as to Ceisne, Sisne, Seisne.

(4) Could you furnish me with some further particulars regarding the Dictionary mentioned in the Pamphlet? If so, I could, perhaps consult it in our libraries over here (Name of author, Etc.)

(5) It is stated therein Cisne or Sesne of Minselles in Normandy. In the Alphabetical Index of French localities, this name does not appear, nor is there any one at all approaching it. Would the above not refer to the "le Cesne" of Menilles, a family which did exist in France?

(6) Beaujeu is a name which in said Index occurs 7 times in various French districts, somewhat distant from each other, all being situated in South-East of France.

(7) I suppose that the coat of arms appearing on the cover of the "Tablet" Pamphlet is the one attributed to the Cessnas. Leaving aside the shape of the shield which strictly speaking is not heraldic, the double eagle does not appear to be French.

To sum up all the above, and with a view of working on lines more or less of certainty, I should like to ask you in what way you wish the matter to proceed.

Either: I would send you in type-written or photostate copy all the particulars ascertained, so as to enable you to compare same with your records.

Or: You would forward me all the informations in your possession, viz. memoranda, genealogical fragments, etc. and restrict the scope of the work. This information would of course, bear on the origin of the Cessnas in America.

So far as I have been able to judge from my examination, it would seem that originally, there were several families of the name of Cesne, Sesne, but this, of course, is only my impression.

Waiting your instructions and with the expression of my regards,

I am, dear Sir,

Yours very truly,

J. S. Willems.

In 1776 Maj. John Cessna then on the Committee of Safety for Bedford County in writing down East for powder and shot, signed his name Cesna. According to above letter he was evidently using the French form.

CHAPTER XIX

Present Address (1935) of Cessnas

J. W. Berryman...Ashland, Kansas
Mary Cessna.............................60 S. 3rd St., Columbus, Ohio
Gwen Cessna Price...Forest, Ohio
Mrs. Virgil Rick.................Bella Vista Apt., Jefferson City, Mo.
(Mrs. Ira W.) Cora Cessna Howeith.........1226 10th St., Greely, Colorado
Mrs. L. T. Thorn...Ravenswood, W. Va.
Gladys Cisney..Richmond Hill, N. Y.
Mrs. Ralph A. Henderson...Sioux City, Ia.
Mrs. Sarah Gump...Everett, Pa.
Mrs. Michael Schuller...Salem, Ohio
Capt. Samuel Williams.............................Fort Leavenworth, Kansas
Mrs. Robert H. Guthrie........532 E. 20th St., No. Portland, Oregon
Charles G. Cissna................2611 N. 12th St., Kansas City, Mo.
Mrs. Geo. P. Douglas.................2424 Park Ave., Minneapolis, Minn.
Mrs. O. C. Fogle...Fairfield, Illinois
Dr. Howard E. Harman...Chillicothe, Ohio
Mrs. J. F. Serowinsky.....................615 Ocean Front, Venice, Calif.
K. W. Cessna.................1729 W. 65 Place, Los Angeles, Calif.
J. M. Cessna...................3215 Moniton, Los Angeles, Calif.
Cliff R. Cessna..................708½ W. 41 Drive, Los Angeles, Calif.
Bernadette Cissna.................4262 W. 1st, Los Angeles, Calif.
Sam Cessna...................1183 W. 39th, Los Angeles, Calif.
H. J. Cessna.....................6410 Mekee, Los Angeles, Calif.
Mrs. Elvira J. Cesena.............745 S. Hope, Los Angeles, Calif.
C. C. Cessna...................564 Franklin, Whittier, Calif.
W. W. Cessna.................358 S. Craig Ave., Pasadena, Calif.
Mrs. Mary Cissna Wilson.........281 E. 14th St., N. Portland, Oregon
Mr. C. Cessna...................Yazoo City, Miss., R. D. 3
Ray C. Cissna.....................................Billingham, Wash.
Clyde V. Cessna...................................Wichita, Kansas
James W. Dougherty...................................Kenton, Ohio
Howard Dougherty...................................Kenton, Ohio
T. C. Cessna.......................................Grinnell, Iowa
F. Brown Cessna.............................Council Bluffs, Iowa
Holmes H. Cessna................................Cumberland, Md.
Bert Sessna.................................White Cloud, Kansas
Mrs. Harry Hummer.................................Latrobe, Pa.
Mrs. J. M. Fink...................................Saxton, Pa.
Eugene Barnett.....................................Bedford, Pa.
Holmes H. Hankin....................................Ottawa, Ill.
Mrs. Belle C. Smith.............875 N. Howard Ave., Salem. Ohio
F. M. Shriver......................................Glenwood, Iowa
C. A. Cessna......................................Uniontown, Pa.
O. M. Cessna...Dows, Iowa
To any Cessna..................................Manhattan, Kansas
To any Cessna..................................Lawrence, Kansas

Present Address of Cessnas

Mrs. Lena G. Chase................................1900 S. Ferry St., Anoka, Minn.
Mrs. E. M. Spivey................................Elizabeth Ave., Winston, N. C.
Mrs. R. C. Russell................................1314 Arch St., Pittsburgh, Pa.
Mrs. N. Cessna Musser................................Pine Bluff, Ark.
E. B. Cessna................................1920 E. 75th St., Cleveland, Ohio
To any Cessna or Relative................................Kansas, Ohio
W. R. Cisney................................470 Vanderbilt Ave., Brooklyn, N. Y.
Mrs. Annie Prosser................................Bedford, Pa.
Mrs. Benj. Ashcom................................Everett, Pa.
Wm. Cunningham................................Enid, Fulton Co., Pa.
Dr. Harry Cunningham................................Juniata, Blair County, Pa.
Clayton Smith................................Bedford, Pa., R. D. No. 4
To any Cessna or Relative................................Nevada, Iowa
To any Cessna or Relative................................Kenton, Ohio
To any Cessna or Relative................................Whiteside Co., Ill.
To any Cessna or Relative................................Keystone, S. Dak.
To any Cessna or Relative................................Rapid City, S. Dak.
To any Cisne or Relative................................Cisne, Ill.
To any Cisne or Relative................................Fairfield, Ill.
To any Cisne or Relative................................Hanson, Nebraska
To any Cisne or Relative................................Smithland, Iowa
To any Cisne or Relative................................Marcus, Iowa
To any Cessna or Relative................................Chillicothe, Mo.
To any Cessna or Relative................................Fulton, Seward Co., Nebr.
To any Cessna or Relative................................Framton, Licking Co., Ohio
To any Cessna or Relative................................Hope, Illinois
To any Cessna or Relative................................Bowling Green, Ohio
To any Cessna or Relative................................Kansas, Ohio
James Sears Campbell or Relative................................Salem, Ohio
J. Paul Huxley................................Salome, Ohio
Ambrose Cessna................................Cumberland, Md.
Duncan Cessna................................Centerville, Bedford Co., Pa.
I. B. Cessna................................Saxton, Pa.
Dr. Russell R. Heim................................4900 Aldrick Ave., So. Minneapolis, Minn.
Carl G. Prior................................Pitts. Term, R. P. O., 11 Ferry St., Pittsburgh, Pa.
To any Cessna or Relative................................Canfield, Ohio
To any Cessna or Relative................................Battle Creek, Mich.
Benton Cessna................................Ellerslie, Md.
John K. Cessna................................Mt. Savage, Md.
Roy Cessna................................Bedford, Pa.
Mrs. John Brice................................Bedford, Pa.
Charlie Cessna................................Bedford, Pa.
To any Cessna or Relative................................Cadiz, Ohio
To any Cessna or Relative................................Fostoria, Ohio
Hon. Harvey Bowers................................Punxsutawney, Pa.
To any Cessna or Relative................................Watseka, Ill.
To any Cessna or Relative................................Hodgensville, Ky.
To any Cessna or Relative................................Burnt Cabin, Fulton Co., Pa.
Mrs. Albert Baldwin................................2505 Octavia St., New Orleans, La.
Mrs. Perry Cessna................................Mt. Savage, Md.
Pauline T. Eldredge................................5620 Howard St., Omaha, Nebr.
E. H. Diehl................................Ipava, Ill.
Mrs. Peter J. Blosser................................Chillicothe, Ohio
Mrs. John E. Zeter................................103 McGowsen Ave., Houston, Texas
R. A. Caldwell................................P. O. Box, 348, Brownsville, Texas
Mrs. Thos. Vance (Fannie Blythe Cessna)................................Orchard Drive, Ames, Iowa

The House of Cessna

Mrs. F. J. Kellogg, (Pearl Cessna)...................................Fowler, Calif.
Mr. J. C. Doty.............................38 Fairmount Ave., Huntingdon, L. I.
Mrs. T. B. Williams........................424 Allegheny St., Hollidaysburg, Pa.
Mr. Paul C. Gerhart...........................4607 Virginia Ave., Dallas, Texas
Mrs. Pres. Metzger........................"Sunnycroft," Johnson City, Tenn.
Miss Edith Gerhart.......................5115 Regent St., Philadelphia, Pa.
Mrs. J. F. Serowinsky........ ....615 Ocean Front, Venice, Calif.
Mrs. R. A. Henderson........................813 25th St., Sioux City, Iowa
John P. Cessna...Diamond, Ohio
Belle Cessna Smith... ....875 N. Howard Ave., Salem, Ohio
J. Paul Huxley...Youngstown, Ohio
Paul Huxley Smith........................875 N. Howard Ave., Salem, Ohio
Mrs. Lynn Shearer...........................114 9th St., N. W., Canton, Ohio
Mrs. Lottie Grove........................3026 Broad Ave., Altoona, Pa.
J. W. DeCessna.......................611 Hartman Bldg., Columbus, Ohio
Mrs. Eleanor Cessna Van Evers.................4043 Park Bldg., San Diego, Calif.
Mrs. Myrtle C. Page..Nampa, Idaho
Hon. Oscar W. Smith.....................735 State St., Santa Barbara, Calif.
Mrs. D. C. Stunkard........................4401 Garrison St., Washington, D. C.
Clyde Cessna...Wichita, Kansas
W. Brown Cessna........................ ....Council Bluffs, Iowa
Reon B. Cessna...Kansas City, Mo.
Hon. J. W. Berryman..Ashland, Kansas
Mrs. Gwen Cessna Price.......................Box 434, Forest, Ohio
Mrs. L. T. Thorn.......................................Ravenswood, W. Va.
J. B. Cessna...East Palestine, Ohio
Mrs. Mary Cissna Wilson...................281 E. 14th St. N., Portland, Oregon
Mrs. Mary M. Gillin.......................................Parkdale, Colorado
Mrs. A. C. Brewer.......................3915 Clover Hill Road, Baltimore, Md.
Miss R. Keller.......................420 Cedar St., Cumberland, Md.
Mrs. Lillian E. Hull.......................424 W. William St., Kendallville, Ind.
Miss Dorothy Martin.......................................Villa Nova, Pa.
Mrs. Anna McNamara.......................3227 Guyson Falls, Baltimore, Md.
Mrs. Julia Cisne Rick.......................649 34th St., N. E., Cedar Rapids, Iowa
J. D. James...Rainsburg, Pa.
Mrs. S. Butler...Cumberland, Md.
To any Jackson...Sioux City, Iowa
To any Record...Glenwood, Iowa
Geo. E. Morgart...Rainsburg, Pa.
To any McGavern...Butte, Montana
Mrs. Carrie Walters...
Hon. Chas. Cessna...Grinnell, Iowa
Thos. Cessna...Rainsburg, Pa.
Samuel Cessna.......................Bedford, Pa., R. D. No. 4
Marshal Cessna...Rainsburg, Pa.
W. A. Cessna...Rainsburg, Pa.
Chester Cessna...Rainsburg, Pa.
Prof. Paul Cessna...Gettysburg, Pa.
H. B. Cessna, Esq...Bedford, Pa.
Mrs. John Minnich.......................................Bedford, Pa.
Mrs. Samuel Orr...Bedford, Pa.
Clyde Cessna...Bedford, Pa.
John T. Cessna...Rainsburg, Pa.
Jennie Cessna...Rainsburg, Pa.
Homer Cessna...Rainsburg, Pa.
Mrs. Edith Mower...Rainsburg, Pa.

Mrs. W. T. Johnson........................7120 Burnett St., Pittsburgh, Pa.
Walter Cessna...Bedford, Pa.
Harry Cessna..Bedford, Pa.
Prof. Arthur Gerhart................................Millersville, S. N. S., Pa.
Wren Cessna...Kansas City
Mr. Cessna...Pueblo, Colorado
Mrs. Nellie Cissna Erickson..............23 Springhaven Road, Wheeling, W. Va.
Mrs. Jas. A. Crawford................219 Main St., Washington C. House, Ohio
Mrs. Mildred Cessna Stoddard...................................Monticello, Ill.
L. A. Clark............................710 West Wash. Ave., Council Bluffs, Iowa
May D. Cissna............................3321 Platt Ave., Lynwood, Calif.
Lamont Stunkard.......................26 Hileman Apt., New Castle, Pa.

An invitation from the author:

In 2018, the Cessna/Cissna/Cisne/Sisney family will have been in America for 300 years. Celebration seems appropriate.

I would like to encourage every branch of the family to plan their own celebration or reunion sometime between now and 2018. Teach our children and grandchildren about the rich heritage we have.

I suggest holding family reunions honoring your oldest living ancestor. Plan it around a birthday, anniversary or date which means the most to your clan.

Gather as much historical data as possible. Record our heritage and leave a record for generations to come. Publicize it and invite other branches of the family to come.

-Bill Cissna
bcissna@aol.com

Made in the USA
Columbia, SC
23 December 2020